Contents

KU-184-196

Acknowledgements

This book has been the outcome of teaching psychology at 'A' level for ten years and I am grateful to all my students who have contributed most considerably to my understanding of the subject. In particular I wish to thank Diane Bowker, Jennifer Gunn and Georgina Meikle for permission to publish their essays. I also wish to thank Mark Johnson and Rachel Stocks for letting me reproduce two of their practicals. I acknowledge the ideas in two practicals written by Annabel Jeremiah and Emma Warren, which helped me with the practical on feedback, and also my colleague Fatima Bhanji, who provided the original idea. For the excellent revision diagram on perception, I am indebted to Georgina Baxter.

I wish most particularly to thank Ann Clynch, who provided valuable advice on an early draft of part of this book and Andrew Conway, who cast his mathematical eye over the statistics section. Finally, I am most grateful to Dax Osborne who provided the excellent cartoons to accompany the statistics section.
All the essay titles with dates were set in that year by the AEB. Any answers or hints on answers are the sole responsibility of the author.

Preface

This book has been written for GCE A-level students, although it will be of use to other students following introductory courses in Psychology. My experience has been that students do not find it easy initially to write essays at this level. This is likely to be increasingly the case with the transition from GCSE work to A-level work. The aim of this book is threefold. First, it provides students with useful and flexible techniques in essay writing. It needs to be stated clearly here, that this is not a model answer book. Such books give the impression that there is only one 'right' answer; they do not tend to show how essays are actually constructed. Second, it provides guidance into how to choose, plan and execute psychology practicals. Third, it gives an overview of the main statistical procedures that are applicable at this level of work.

The approach in this book is to analyse questions in such a way that the student is provided with a basic framework for an answer. This can be developed into a full essay. The preparation for essays, writing essays for homework and also under test conditions, are dealt with, as are questions of revision and dealing with examinations.

Suggestions for practicals are given. A detailed guide to planning and writing up practicals is provided, along with two examples of actual student practicals fully written up and annotated. This book does not attempt to provide a complete coverage of statistics. This is already effectively done in a number of suitable texts. However, it does give the student an introduction and reference to the main procedures, as well as examples of questions on statistics and methodology.

To avoid cluttering up the text with footnotes, full references are not given on authors whose work can be readily located in the major text books.

Introduction

In order to successfully complete your course in Psychology, you will have to develop two distinct skills. The first is to be able to write essays on given topics, under time pressure. The second, is to carry out a number of practical studies and to write them up in an appropriate manner. In order to effectively undertake practical work, you will also need to develop some facility with statistics. This book is designed to help you develop these skills.

Many students fail to do justice to themselves by a lack of essay writing skills and poor examination technique. While this guide includes a number of specific essays, its purpose is not to provide 'right answers'. Rather, it will show how to prepare for and effectively answer examination questions. Two basic techniques are used with regard to the essays. The first is to provide some examples of essays written by students under test conditions. Generally these are of a high standard, and show what can be achieved. These essays are annotated with comments to highlight their particular strengths and weaknesses. The second approach is to take actual 'A' level questions and to try to show in a visual way the relationship between the various arguments suggested by each question. To do this, 'thought-webs' or 'mind-maps' are used. Students have found this a very flexible way of setting out ideas, which helps them to structure their arguments in the answer.

A wide range of questions has been chosen to touch on most aspects of an introductory course. While no book of this length can be fully comprehensive, most of the major issues in psychology are considered.

The answers given in this book to questions are just suggestions. There are many ways in which questions can be answered. What this book seeks to demonstrate are some of the techniques behind the construction of good answers.

With regard to practical work, this book seeks to make explicit the relationship between the design of an experiment, the type of data generated and the statistical procedures that are then necessary. Guidance is given in the special style of writing that is appropriate for practical work. Particular attention is given to the problem of undertaking observation studies, and how data from such studies should be recorded and presented.

Using the book
Firstly, with regard to essays, study the questions in the area that you are dealing with. When you are set an essay, follow the guidelines that are set out in the next section on the research and planning for essays. Practise making detailed plans before you start writing. This cannot be emphasised enough. In carefully thinking through a plan you deepen your understanding of an issue and it becomes both easier to write about and more memorable. The thought-web approach to planning is particularly helpful, as it enables you to overview at a glance, the relationship between all the arguments you will be presenting. It is also a technique that is a considerable aid when it comes to revision.

Study the full-length essays that have been included, to see the way in which the writers have structured their ideas and linked them to the question. Try to incorporate any good points of technique in your own essays.

When the exam approaches then this book can be used as an aid in revision. You can use the questions to practise exam-length essays which can be checked against the detailed plans provided.

Secondly, for practical work, this book provides step by step guidance in planning practicals. If this is followed, then the writing up of the practical report will be made relatively easy. Most of the main concepts that involve statistics are covered, and a chart is provided to assist with choosing the most appropriate statistical test. There is also detailed guidance notes on how practicals can be written up.

Again, study the full length examples that are given, and make a note of any points of good practice that you can incorporate into your own work.

The cartoons and diagrams given in the practical and statistical sections, are designed to illustrate some of the fundamental concepts. Try to grasp their significance. If you can understand these basic building blocks of the statistical method early in your course, then you will find that statistics are much more straightforward than they may appear at first.

Research for essays and practicals

Your success in the A-level examination will depend upon how effectively you can answer the questions that are set. Your ability to do this will depend on how well you have prepared yourself over the two years of your course. Coursework essays that have been well researched will deepen your understanding of Psychology and provide good material to revise from.

Good practicals also require sound research skills. It is necessary to gather relevant material to provide the background to the research you are doing, and also to provide a clear context for your study. Being methodical and accurate in this work, and developing the ability to summarise well, will be of considerable value to you in this field as well as others.

Research

If you are preparing for a specific essay title, or if you are researching a particular problem relating to practical work, then make sure that you understand the implications of what you are looking into before you start your research. You need to 'decode' essay questions sufficiently to make sure that your research is on the right lines. Similarly, with practicals, you need to be sure that you gather material which relates to the variables that you are considering. For example, if you are comparing arts and science students, then you will need to look for material that is relevant to the study of arts and science, as variables. If you can find no material, then you may need to reformulate your study. It is important that your practicals are related – at least to a significant degree – to recognised psychological research.

Use of texts

There are a considerable number of texts that you may have access to. You will not have time to read all the material in all of them. Make good use of the table of contents and the index in order to find the relevant pages for your particular field of interest. Skim through unfamiliar material, first to get an overview of what is being said, and secondly to locate parts that are of particular relevance to your needs. Make brief notes *in your own words*. Do not copy verbatim out of the texts. If you rephrase in your own words, you have to think about what you are reading. This will tend to deepen your understanding – and you will use the material more effectively in your essays and practicals. Make sure that you record the important details (names, dates, statistics).

Use of other books

You may find specialist books on specific topics in the library. Try not to get lost in detail, but use these books to provide fuller information on aspects of the essay or practical that you are doing. Again the index and contents pages will prove invaluable for saving time. It is important that you go beyond the one or two main text books that you use in order to do well in the final examination.

References

For your practicals you will need to give references. These should be done to a consistent format. As you will often use one or two texts for most of your information you will need to record more than just the author and the title. You need to be able to show what information came from what source. For example:

Dobson et al, *Understanding Psychology* , Wiedenfeld and Nicolson, 1981:
    Collins and Quillian (pp 128–130)
    Bower (p 131)
    Craik (p 126)
Atkinson, Atkinson and Hilgard, *Introduction to Psychology*, (8th Edition), Harcourt Brace Jovanovich, 1983:
    Bower (p 234)
    Bower and Clark (p 241)
    Murdock (p 245)

Other sources

You should look out for programmes on television that are relevant to the field of Psychology. They are not uncommon, and will often prove highly informative. For programmes that are clearly of relevance to you, it is helpful to make a few notes on the main points that are made, and the key names involved.

Note taking

Your notes should be clear, with sufficient detail, but not over-long. You need to record the essence of the argument and the key points of particular studies or theories. Some illustrative material to back up arguments is important but don't get lost in detail.

Set out your notes clearly. Even though you will be writing an essay based on them, or introducing a practical, they may still prove valuable for revision later in the course. Make liberal use of headings, subheadings, underlining and colour. These will make your notes clearer and more interesting to read. If you look at the memory section in Psychology text-books, you will see that use of interesting layout and colour is one way of improving memorability.

Cards

Many students find that writing summaries of studies on cards can prove to be very useful. It is strongly recommended that you do this right from the start of your course. For each main study and theory you should produce a card. This card should have the main points about the study, the author and the date. Material on cards can be easily manipulated when you plan your essay. They will also be invaluable for revision later.

Planning for essays

Essays packed with good material, which is presented haphazardly, will never gain very much credit. While planning what you are going to write may not be easy, especially early on in the course, it will serve to clarify the ideas that are being written about. The plan should reflect the broad outline of the argument being presented. Before a plan can be made for a given question, the question needs to be analysed. To accomplish this, underline the key words in the question or title. Then try to restate in your own words what the question is saying. Scribble down, in any order, the main points that you wish to include in your answer. These can be worked later into a structured plan. Note whether the question is asking you to 'discuss' or 'explain' or 'evaluate' or 'compare' or 'give evidence', and whether you are expected to 'be critical'.

It may seem like stating the obvious, but a good essay will have a beginning, a middle and an end. There are a number of ways in which you might structure your answer. Here are two:
1 The 'evaluation'
   Introduction, with main terms defined
   Development of ideas, with illustrations and criticisms
   Conclusion in relation to the question set
2 The 'debate'
   Introduction, with main issues outlined
   One line of argument (with theory and evidence)
   The opposing line of argument (with theory and evidence)
   Discussion and conclusion
While the overall plan will probably conform to one of these patterns, the detailed structure of the arguments may be more complex. The use of 'thought-webs' or 'mind-maps' can be most helpful in allowing you to build up your plan around certain ideas. This technique is illustrated in the next section. The finished plan for a coursework essay should show where the main arguments and ideas are to be introduced, and what theorists and studies are to be mentioned at various points. Even under examination conditions a brief plan can prove invaluable, and can help ensure that the essay has a good structure.

Planning for practicals

This will be dealt with in detail later on in this text, as there is a format for writing practicals which can be followed quite closely. For the introduction and the discussion sections of the practical, the same ideas about planning apply. It is often necessary to cover a lot of material in relatively few words. This requires you to be clear about what you want to say, and the best order in which to say it. A clear plan will prove invaluable.

Writing psychology essays

Both the examination and coursework essays are used to test your ability to describe and analyse psychological theories and the findings that support or refute them; to make comparisons of theories; to select and weigh evidence in support of an argument; and to express critical judgements.

Lack of success at 'A' level often comes from the result of either:

a) writing at a level appropriate for GCSE, that is factually based, but not bridging the gap to 'A' level work, which requires a greater emphasis on the relationship between theory and actual research; or

b) the all-and-sundry answer that combines assertions, common sense, with nuggets of psychological research, not effectively related to the question.

The highest grades are achieved by those who are able to amass a considerable amount of information relating to a topic, in an orderly and coherent way. Such essays exhibit a clear line of argument, with each part related to the one before and the one that follows. The essay rests on a sound factual basis and also develops and discusses the appropriate concepts and theories.

Often a major weakness of essays done at home, or under test conditions, is irrelevance. You must answer the question that is set. Make a plan. When the plan is complete then check that it does actually answer the question. In a woodwork room in a school there was a sign on the wall – 'think twice, cut once'. The same principle applies to essay writing. Checking your plan against the question means that you will not go off at a tangent. When actually writing, check frequently that the points you are making and the arguments you are developing, are clearly linked to the main issues in the question.

The coursework essay

The purpose of this type of work, is to enable you to present in your own words, the ideas and arguments relating to a particular issue or question. Generally such an essay is set after you have gone over the issue in class. It is a chance for you to re-express the ideas that have been presented to you. By so doing you have the opportunity to really grasp the significance of what you have been taught, and to move from knowledge about a topic, largely contained in your notes, to understanding. A topic, when really understood, is much easier to remember. Consequently, you can see the coursework essay, if worked on effectively, can be of real value in preparing you for the examination (and, incidentally, helping you to grasp some of the main issues in psychology for their own sake). The ability to present complex arguments is a valuable skill in itself. Writing essays can help you to develop this communication skill if you keep in mind certain principles:

1 You should prepare for the essay adequately. Don't let it be a 'last minute job', accomplished amid the detritus of a coffee bar, on the morning that it is due! Equally, the best essays are not those written with one eye on the TV.

2 Make a detailed plan. Know where you are going to put the various arguments before you start. The plan gives you an overview of what you are going to write at various stages. This means that each section is a coherent part of the whole.

3 Make your opening relevant. You should commence with an issue, idea or finding that is of particular relevance to the question that you are tackling. This should indicate the angle or direction that you will follow.

4 Link the main stages of your argument. Give signposts that the reader can follow.

5 Imagine that you are writing for an intelligent person, who is well read but not familiar with this topic. In other words give sufficient detail, without having to go into all the minutiae.

6 Generally allow each idea or study, a paragraph of its own. Then link the paragraphs together, so that the argument flows.

7 Finally, make sure that as you approach the end, you round off what you are saying. Establish a conclusion, or at least sum up what you see as being the balance of the arguments that you have presented. The conclusion allows you to critically review the relative merits of the various arguments in the essay.

The coursework essay should be comprehensive in its coverage of a topic. This will help both in understanding the issues and also as a revision aid later. You need therefore to be accurate in the details that you quote. Make an effort to explain and discuss the theories and ideas that you present. Often the essay will be the final piece of work you do on a topic before you prepare for the examination. So it is when you write the essay that you should invest the time and effort to ensure that you really understand what you are writing about.

The examination essay

The purpose of the examination essay is to test your knowledge of psychology, your understanding of the theories and your ability to give clear expression to your ideas. Your purpose in writing the essay is to score high marks. This you will do by showing that you really comprehend the question and then providing a well-organised and informed answer. This whole book is designed to help you accomplish this, but here are some pointers that can help.

Always read the question through at least twice to ensure that you really understand what is actually being asked. The folly of answering a question that has not been set is obvious, and results in much wasted effort and heartache. Then go through the question again and underline the key terms. This will ensure that you will not miss any vital points. Then make a plan. This will not be elaborate, as under examination conditions you will not have the time. But it should be adequate. It is surprising how much you can get down on paper in two or three minutes, and it is time very well spent. When completed, check your plan against the question to ensure that you have answered what has actually been set.

There are three elements to bear in mind when writing an examination essay: structure, content and style. The *structure* of the essay refers to the way in which you organise the argument. It should be logical, clear and appropriate. Your argument should unfold through linked paragraphs, and the main sections of the essay should form a coherent whole. The *content* refers to the substance of the essay. This must be appropriate and in sufficient detail. It relates to the level of conceptual development in the essay. In other words, how far the main concepts implicit in the arguments are explained and developed. Also, it is concerned with the ability to set what you write in a theoretical context. The *style* is your own way of expressing ideas. The essay should be as clear as possible, but there is room for a little ingenuity and originality in the presentation.

In the next section we will start by looking in detail at how an essay is planned and written.

Constructing an essay

Outline and evaluate the Piagetian view of child development (1986)

Analysis of the question

The first step in tackling a question is to consider the key words and phrases. These can be underlined for greater clarity.

<u>Outline</u> and <u>evaluate</u> the <u>Piagetian</u> view of <u>child development</u>

The question can now be analysed in more detail.

Outline   this implies giving an overview picking out the main points of Piaget's theories and experiments.

evaluate   this prompts us to consider the value of Piaget's work. What is of lasting significance? What aspects have been criticised? What is the status of his work?

Piagetian   the focus in this essay is Piaget. What is the particular contribution he has made – and what is implied by 'Piagetian'?

Child Development   this gives us our subject matter – namely all that is encompassed by the term 'child development.'

Planning the question

When preparing an essay for class, a plan is valuable. It provides a check list to make sure that what you are going to cover is adequate, and most important, will answer the question. A brief plan is very helpful even when writing under examination conditions.

As a start a list of points could be made. Initially, write them down as they occur. They can be organised later. At this stage go for completeness.

Piaget's theory	*Empirical Studies*	*Critical points*
Biologist	Object permanence	Bower
Evolutionary theory	Conservation	Donaldson
Cognitive development	Mountain experiment	Hughes
Four main stages	Beaker problem	Gelman and Gallistel
Moral development	Play	'Naughty Teddy'
Egocentrism	Rules and morals	Language use
His methodology		Bruner
Assimilation		
Schemas		

This initial list may be added to as you continue your planning. However, the purpose of an essay is not to put down everything you know or can find out about a topic, rather it is to effectively answer the question drawing on relevant information to support your argument. You are now in a position to move on to a plan for the essay. This can be in the form of a mind-map or thought-web, or a sequential list. We will illustrate both here. In exam conditions only a brief version of these will be possible.

The plan should pick out the fundamental structure of the argument that you wish to make. If this is clear to you, then your essay will gain in coherence and relevance.

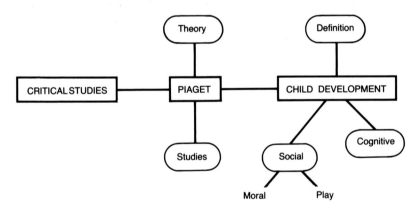

This initial plan indicates the three aspects of the answer, namely:

1 what is child development

2 what is Piaget's contribution to our understanding of it, and

3 what critical evaluation has been made of Piaget's work.

A fuller plan would look like this:

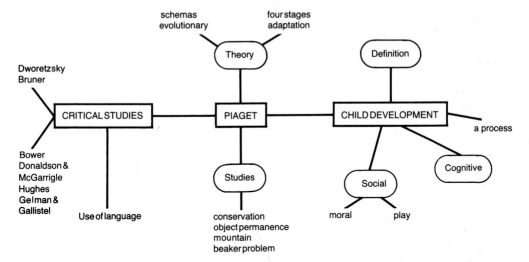

The value of a map, like this is that the whole argument can be seen at a glance, and the relationship between parts of the argument made apparent. However, it is also quite acceptable to do a straightforward linear plan. Use whichever method you find suits you best.

Child development
    Definition
    Cognitive development – a process
    Social development – moral; play

Piaget
    His theory
    – Biological basis; evolutionary
    – Schemas
    – Adaptation
    – Four stages

Studies
    – Observation
    – Object permanence
    – Conservation experiments
    – Mountain – egocentrism
    – Beaker problem-formal

Critical studies
    – Bower – object permanence
    – Donaldson and McGarrigle – Naughty teddy
    – Hughes – police doll and boy doll
    – Gelman and Gallistel – number
    – Use of language
    – Dworetzsky
    – Bruner

Concluding evaluation

What follows is one possible answer to this question. This is the only 'model answer' in the book and it should be understood that there would be many other ways to deal with this question just as adequately.

As will be the practice later in the book, a brief commentary is provided to explain why the question is being approached in this way. The length of the essay is what could be achieved by most 'A' level students under exam conditions.

Piaget, a Swiss biologist, turned his attention to cognitive development in children, after working with Binet on the development of IQ tests. While his primary interest was cognitive development, he considered other aspects of child development including moral development and the role of play.**(1)** The term development implies two aspects. The first, is a maturational component, with a biological basis. The second, is a learned component. Piaget was concerned with the interaction between these two aspects. He investigated the process of the development of intelligence and moral thought.**(2)**

(1) The introduction is directly related to the question and lays the groundwork for explaining what 'Piagetian' means as well as picking out what will be covered later.

There are four basic stages in the Piagetian approach to child development. These are the sensorimotor stage (0–2 years); the pre-operational stage (2–7 years); the concrete operational stage (7–11 years); and finally the formal operational stage (11 years and over). These stages are discontinuous in the sense that they mark quite distinctly different ways of representing and understanding the world.**(3)** Piaget was intrigued by how the child made sense of the world. He explained this in terms of schemas, or internal representations, and the process of adaptation. Adaptation consists of two complementary activities. Assimilation, which is where experience of the environment is absorbed into already existing schemas, and accomodation, where new experience leads to disequilibrium and can only be dealt with by a change in schemas.**(4)**

(2) The first part of the plan has now been dealt with, albeit in a very succinct manner.

(3) The temptation here is to write at length on the stages. However, only as much detail as is necessary for the question need be given.

(4) Again, a degree of Piaget's 'pure theory' needs to be covered, but can be dealt with briefly.

Piaget's theory is based on extensive observational studies, which he carried out with children. It is this firm foundation of empirical support that has made his work so influential, even if some of the details of his findings have been criticised.**(5)**

(5) It is important to mention Piaget's methodology.

In the first four months of the sensori-motor stage the child has no sense of object permanence. It is a case of 'out of sight and out a mind'. Bower (1972), however, disputes this and showed that, with the right experimental technique, a child will track an object and show surprise if it does not re-appear after passing behind a screen.**(6)**

Many of Piaget's experiments were concerned with conservation – of mass, of volume and of number. He demonstrated that in the pre-operational stage a child will perceive liquid poured from a short, fat glass to a long thin one, as having in-

(6) Again, this is a very brief summary, both of Piaget's ideas and that of Bower. The choice has been made here to make contrasts as the essay unfolds, rather than deal first with Piaget and then with his critics. Either approach will do.

creased. The child conceives that there is 'more' liquid in the thinner glass. In other words he/she cannot conserve volume. Similar findings were established with regard to mass (using Plasticine) and number (using coins or counters). Children up to the age of seven tended to see change of shape or form as indicating some substantial change.**(7)**

While the basic premise, that children do not have a clear schema for conservation at this age is broadly accepted, there have been critical studies. Donaldson and McGarrigle (1979) used a 'Naughty Teddy' to make the rearrangements. They found the child would show conservation much younger with the Naughty Teddy than with the experimenter. Using sugar mice, and simple sleight-of-hand, Gelman and Gallistel (1978) showed that children had much more sense of number than Piaget had given them credit for, even if they could not count in the accepted adult way. Donaldson (1970) suggested that the very language used in these experiments could confuse the children.**(8)** During this period a notable feature of the child's thought is egocentrism, which will be considered next.

The child, says Piaget, is egocentric and tends to see things from his/her own standpoint. This he demonstrated with the classic mountain view experiment. He showed that pre-operational children tended to assume that a doll, looking at a model mountain scene, would see the same view that they did. Subsequent studies, notably that of Hughes (1984) using an interesting cross of walls, suggested otherwise. In Hughes' study children had to hide a 'boy-doll' from 'policemen dolls'. He showed that $3\frac{1}{2}$ to 5 year olds were successful, in working out the policeman's viewpoint, 90% of the time.**(9)**

In the next stage, of concrete operations, Piaget demonstrated that the child becomes able to classify to a much greater extent. However, certain logic problems can only be solved with physical objects and cannot be worked out mentally until about the age of 11.

At 11 the child begins to achieve formal operations. It can now manipulate ideas, and approach scientific problems in a logical way. This Piaget demonstrated with a simple experiment involving working out how to mix various combinations of colourless liquids. The child who has achieved formal operations will not be random in his/her procedure.

Work by Dworetzsky (1981) has supported Piaget's, showing that the adolescent can think hypothetically. Other studies (notably Wason (1965) and Dulitt (1972)) have shown many adults never appear to achieve this stage.

While Piaget's main focus has been cognitive development, he has applied his ideas in other areas as well.**(10)** He suggests the child goes through distinct stages of moral development,

(7) It is possible to give brief sketches to illustrate these experiments, but only where they will save time in writing.

(8) At this point the section on conversation is completed as far as time and space allows. A link needs to be made to the next idea, which is egocentrism.

(9) Exam essays do not need to be packed with facts and figures, but some should be learned. Also roughly when people did their studies should be remembered.

(10) Here again is an explicit link, so the essay does not jump from point to point.

which link to his/her understanding of rules. The moral judgement of the child changes as he/she comes to be able to
understand intention. Piaget tested this idea using hypothetical
stories. His work has been extended by Kohlberg who developed
a more elaborate theory of six stages.

Piaget has shown that children's play goes through similar
stages. Overall, his theory appears to hold together well. It has
formed the basis of other theoretical developments – like that
of Bruner and Kohlberg. It also has been very influential on the
profession of teaching, especially in the structuring of activities
in the primary school.**(11)**

While other theorists like Freud and Skinner have raised very
different issues to those of Piaget, his work on cognitive development stands up well to his critics.

(11) The essay need
not end with a
summary, but rather
should conclude in
relation to the actual
question.

Critically discuss the use of the scientific method in Psychology (1988)

This is *not* asking 'is Psychology a Science?' but rather, 'how applicable
is the *scientific method* to psychology'. The question asks for a *critical*
discussion, which implies that it is debatable whether psychology as a
whole can usefully adopt the scientific method. A further implication
is that the idea of the scientific method itself, needs to be considered
critically. This can be reflected in our initial plan.

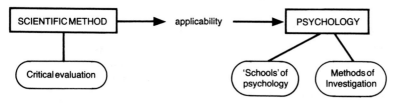

The answer will contain two basic threads. The first is (a) assessing
the usefulness of the scientific method to 'schools' of psychology (eg
behaviourism, cognitive psychology) and (b) considering the degree of
scientificity of various methods of investigation used by psychologists.
The second thread is to look critically at the concept of scientific
method, recognising that various writers see the concept of a 'scientific
method' as a problem.

The elaborated 'map' or 'web of ideas' could now look like this:

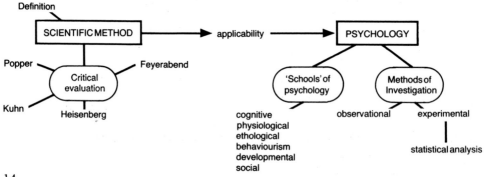

A clear definition of what is generally assumed to be the scientific method is required. This could emphasise the role of theory, experimentation, objectivity, statistical analysis of data and law like generalisations. This orthodox definition would then be contrasted with various schools or approaches that constitute psychology. Physiological psychology and behaviourism would fit closely with the model. Cognitive psychology, could be more of a problem because of the non-material nature of the concepts (thought, memory, moral development). Yet the experimental method is often rigorously applied in cognitive psychology (eg Bruner's work on thinking or many of the studies on memory). Developmental psychology, ethology and social psychology as well as psychoanalysis, pose distinct problems ranging from the use of observation to the degree to which their concepts are testable.

This could form a link to either a discussion of Popper and falsifiability or to the issues concerned with laboratory experiments in psychology as opposed to observation.

One problem with observations is the potential influence of the observer on the observed. In the laboratory situation there is the difficulty with human subjects of experimenter effects and demand characteristics. Heisenberg's uncertainty principle would suggest this criticism faces all science and not just psychology.

Finally, both Kuhn (with his idea of paradigms) and Feyerabend (with his argument that science is actually anarchic) provide a critique of the idea that there is an immutable 'scientific method' that is objective.

Compare and contrast two approaches to the study of personality

There are many different personality theories. A question like this is fairly open ended because it allows you to choose which aspects of personality theory you wish to concentrate on. You are advised therefore to choose two theories that are sufficiently different to provide a real contrast. Eysenck's trait theory provides a *nomothetic* example (dealing with differences in individual characteristics). This could be compared to Freudian theory, which is *idiographic* (focusing on the effect of individual life experience).

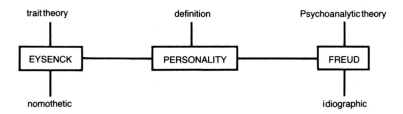

There are two obvious ways in which the essay can now be approached. The first is to deal completely with one or other theory. This would then be followed by the second theory, emphasising salient points of difference. The second would compare each theory in relation to a series of points (eg model of man, measurement, classification of types,

15

evidence etc). This is a more sophisticated method but it requires careful planning and thought. Even with the first method, the various
points of contrast do need to be considered before the essay is started.

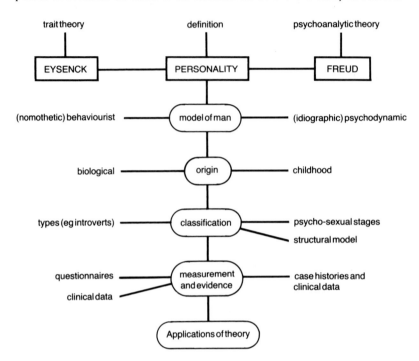

The two theories rest on a quite different conceptualisation of the nature of the human being. Eysenck's model draws on the tradition of
behaviourism, with its biological basis and ideas of conditioning.
Freud's approach to personality, although it has a biological aspect
(with the concept of libido), emphasises the impact of childhood experience during the various psychosexual stages. The way each theory
classifies personality types needs to be considered in sufficient detail.
With Eysenck there are links to the classical typology of Galen
(melancholic, phlegmatic etc). This he combined with the ideas of in-
troversion, extroversion, neuroticism and psychoticism. The oral, anal
and phallic stages of Freudian theory require brief explanation, as does
the structural approach to personality emphasising the Id, Ego and
Super-ego. It is not necessary to go into great detail on these aspects.
   More space should rather be given to the way in which these personality types are used. The various inventories developed by Eysenck
should be explained and the clinical evidence for the Freudian types
should be assessed. There is biological evidence for Eysenck's theory
(eg introverts showing higher cortical activity – Gale, 1981). There is
also persuasive evidence for some aspects of the types suggested by
Freud (eg on the anal personality – Kline, 1981). There is little
evidence that such personality types are caused by childhood experience, like toilet training.

A further way of making a comparison would be to look at how far the theories have contributed to clinical practice. Eysenccks's methods although very reliable, have a very narrow application. Freud's theory is much less reliable, but remains very influential in clinics. If time and space allow, some brief discussion of other related theories would be appropriate, where they throw light on the debate.

Discuss how evidence from visual deprivation studies has helped psychologists to understand the process of visual perception (1987)

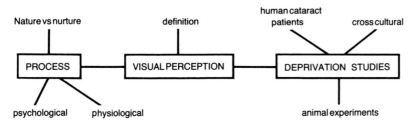

The phrase 'process of visual perception' suggests both the idea of sequence and activity. The point should be made that the process can be influenced by both heredity (nature) and environment (nurture). Deprivation studies have been used to establish the degree to which visual perception is innate. What is meant by 'deprivation' should be clearly defined, because it arguably goes beyond laboratory studies of animals and could embrace cross-cultural studies.

After clearly defining the parameters of the debate in this essay, certain studies illustrating aspects of the argument need to be presented. Sufficient relevant detail should be given and the crucial steps in the debate highlighted. The problem of separating out the psychological activity of perception from the physiological factors can be illustrated with Weiskrantz' (1956) criticisms of Reisen's (1947) work. The various experiments on cats (Hubel and Weisel; Blakemore; Leventhal and Hirsch; Held and Hein) are relevant.

Natural deprivation occurs in human patients who have had cataracts from birth. The removal of these cataracts allows the process of perception to be studied (Von Senden; Hebb; Gregory and Wallace).

While it may be stretching the definition of deprivation a bit, cross-cultural studies could be *briefly* mentioned. The lack of certain features in both the physical and social environment can be shown to influence perception. The effect of poverty on perception of coin size is a case in point.

The effective answer to this question will evaluate the relative status of the evidence presented, and make clear links between the results of the studies and the concept of the *process* of perception.

Consider whether evidence justifies a distinction between short-term and long-term memory (1985)

Here the focus is on how far experimental *evidence* provides *justification* for those theories (eg Atkinson-Shiffrin) which suggest memory involves distinct stages. An alternative approach argues that much of this evidence can be explained as a by-product of information processing.

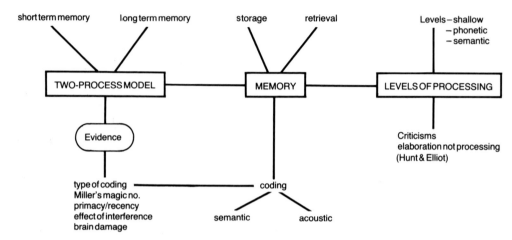

A clear definition of what is meant by the terms short term memory (STM) and long term memory (LTM) is necessary. The evidence of this model, developed by Atkinson and Shiffrin could be presented prior to the extensions and modifications of the model. Some consideration would be given to the term 'justification'; what evidence would or indeed could, establish such a distinction? Can the same evidence support an alternative model? The fact that this is a 'model' and the evidence does not *demonstrate* a physiological structure should be noted. A brief review of the evidence for the STM and LTM hypotheses will be necessary. The development of the concept of working memory (Baddeley, 1986) has extended this idea of the STM. Similarly Tulving (1972) has differentiated the LTM with its semantic and episodic components. The major alternative to their model is the levels of processing theory of Craik and Lockhart (1972). Evidence for this should be evaluated in the light of criticisms (eg Baddeley, 1978).

What have psychologists learned about the nature of prejudice? How useful has this knowledge been in attempts to reduce prejudice? (1987)

The question has two parts, and each part needs to be tackled adequately. An effective answer will demonstrate how specific approaches to studying prejudice have informed approaches to its reduction. If the causes of prejudice are to be found fundamentally in interpersonal interactions, then change may be possible. If, however, the causes are 'deeper', at a personality level, then change will be much less easy to accomplish.

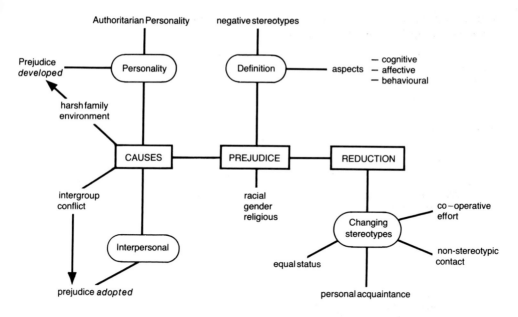

The personality theories of prejudice, suggest it is the outcome of a particular style of upbringing. This results in the authoritarian personality and the closed-minded individual (Adorno; Rokeach). Eysenck's tough-minded and tender-minded traits even suggest a possible biological cause. These approaches suggest prejudice is *developed* in the early years of life. The result is a 'prejudice prone personality' which would be very difficult to change. Brief instances of these theories would be alluded to. The social psychological theories that see prejudice arising from intergroup conflict offer more hope for change. The classic study of group competition by Sherif (1961) would be contrasted with more recent work by Tyerman and Spencer (1983). Tajfel (1941) indicates that mere membership of a group is sufficient to produce prejudice. There appears to be a tendency for prejudice to be *adopted* or learned. This may be through conformity to group power (Pettigrew, 1971) or the impact of the mass media. A final explanation, scapegoating, offers less hope as this suggests that when we are frustrated we will tend to displace our aggression onto an out-group.

Reduction of prejudice has come about through the application of the interpersonal theories. By encouraging contact between groups of equal status, psychosis is reduced (Deutsch and Collins, 1951). However, recent research by Stephen (1978) suggests this may not be so. Encouraging personal acquaintance enabling co-operative contact has been tried (Aronson, 1978) but with only modest success. The visibility of non-stereotypic examples may also reduce prejudice. Each of these arguments can be applied in relation to race, colour and religion.

Using experimental evidence, evaluate the contribution of attribution theory to our understanding of behaviour (1986)

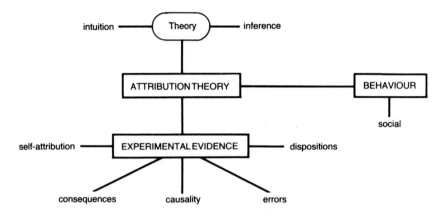

Fritz Heider's (1958) work originated this field of study and deserves a mention. He investigated how people *infer* the intentions of others to explain their behaviour. The alternative 'intuitional' or global gestalt model could be alluded to but need not be explored in depth. As *experimental* evidence is asked for, the essay should highlight this aspect in the evaluations, rather than remaining a theoretical or conceptual discussion. However, the conceptual issues should form a framework for the answer.

One way the essay could be organised would be around central concepts like dispositions, causality, consequences etc. The various studies would be considered then in relation to these ideas, while recognising they are not necessarily mutually exclusive categories. Dispositions might be considered first. As experimental evidence is particularly asked for, theoretical models like Harold Kelley's (1967) Co-variation explanation, should just be outlined. Empirical assessments of it need to be covered in more detail (eg Zuckerman; Kruglanski; Garland). The correspondent inference theory and experiments of Jones and Davis (1965) also relate to dispositions.

The attribution of causality for behaviour in relation to external and internal causes has been studied by Harvey et al (1976), by Nisbett and Ross (1980) and Lalljee (1982). Experimental studies of self-attribution (eg Berglas and Jones 1978) and the studies of errors in the process of attribution (eg Kulik 1983) could be considered. The research by Wallster (1966) which investigated people's attributions of motives to the driver in an accident with varying severity of consequences, introduces an important additional line of analysis.

In an essay like this, avoid getting bogged down in lists of studies. One representative piece of research in each conceptual area is sufficient, if it is reviewed critically. The relevance of the research must be made explicit and can be supported by supplementary evidence if you have time.

Compare and contrast operant and classical conditioning (1985)

When asked to 'compare and contrast' two aspects of psychology, then the main focus of the essay is on the similarities and differences of these two aspects, rather than criticisms from outside. This question requires a structure that will enable this to be done in a coherent way.

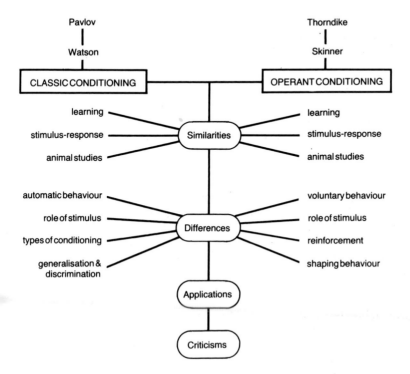

There is a vast amount of material that could be covered in an essay like this, and some careful selection should be made. Under exam conditions it would not be possible to produce a plan as elaborate as the one given above, but the key points of historical background and definition, similarities, differences, applications and criticisms would provide a broad framework for the answer. The similarities would include a basic concept of the nature of the human being and a reductionist approach to explanations, which is connected to the tendency to study animals (although the studies of humans and the applications to learning and therapy deserve a mention). In the mind map above, ideas that could be compared and contrasted have been linked. The differences revolve particularly around the idea of choice and voluntary action. Some criticisms can be mentioned as a similarity, in the sense that some apply equally to both (eg reductionism). Others apply more to operant conditioning theory (eg the role of insight in learning, creativity, and explanations of language learning).

To what extent is the study of animals helpful in understanding human behaviour? (1984)

Open-ended questions like this require careful thought if the answer is not to ramble. A structure needs to be imposed. Clearly, comparative psychology provides much useful information for understanding certain aspects of human behaviour, but not all. Understanding of this sort is a form of reductionism, which would be briefly alluded to. This could be linked to the idea of 'competing models of man', some of which see man as basically an animal (behaviourism) and some of which do not (humanism).

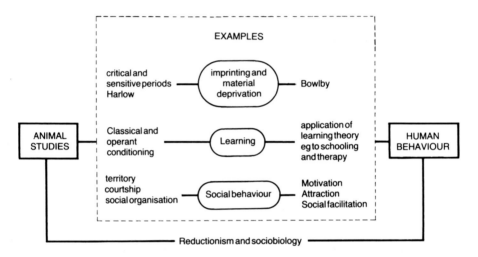

One way to organise an answer, is around specific areas of psychology where animal studies have been used to highlight human behaviour. In addition to those in the mind map, physiology, perception and language learning, could also be considered. It is not sufficient to just list studies or findings, but to show why these animal studies aid our understanding of human behaviour. Some differentiation needs to be made between where animal studies show real congruence with human behaviour (eg at the physiological level) and where human behaviour may need to be explained in human terms (eg much social psychology, Kelly's Personal Construct Theory, Jung on individuation, Erikson's stages etc). A consideration of sociobiology, when one of the highest aspects of human behaviour (altruism) is explained by the basic building block of life (namely genes) could provide a conclusion. Some degree of *assessment* about how helpful animal studies are should be made.

Discuss whether sleep and dreaming are necessary (1983)

This is a straightforward question that revolves around a careful analysis of the implication of the word 'necessary'. Is there evidence that human beings can survive without sleep or dreaming? The terms sleep and dreaming can be approached through a brief discussion of

22

the concept of consciousness. In sleep there is reduced conscious aware-ness. With dreams the awareness is of an inner subjective experience. The danger in this essay is loss of relevance through going off at a tangent on either the physiology of sleep or studies of dreaming *per se.*

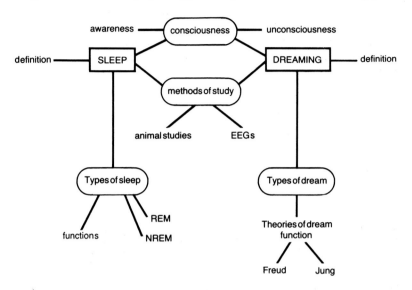

Both sleep and dreaming are aspects of consciousness. The electro-encephalographic (EEG) studies of sleep have revealed the different levels of consciousness involved. The types of brain wave associated with different types of sleep should be explained and a differentiation made between the REM and NREM sleep patterns. Animal studies, and the physiological factors associated with sleeping, indicate the in-voluntary and evolutionary aspects of this behaviour. They suggest both sleep and dreaming aid the species to survive.

The studies that investigate the necessity for both sleep and dreams, are mainly of the effects of deprivation. The need for NREM sleep can be approached in terms of theories about why sleep has evolved (eg Meddis, 1977; Rogers, 1981) and 'restoration theories' which suggest the need for sleep to restore the physical organism (eg Webb, 1975; Oswald, 1974). The studies of REM sleep, raise more complex issues and make a link to dreaming. NREM sleep on its own does not seem to be sufficient for physiological well-being. Cats appear to suffer if deprived of REM sleep (Jouvet, 1967). Dement (1960) found humans tended to hallucinate when not allowed to sustain REM sleep. The idea of REM sleep and associated dreaming, as enabling the brain/mind to process the day's experience, appears well founded (eg Evans and Newman, 1964). This idea connects with the more psychoanalytic approach. The work of Freud and Jung could be touched on in this context.

Discuss the interaction of cognitive and physiological factors during emotional states (1985)

This question allows the careful contrast between three distinct models of the nature and origin of emotional states. Before these are outlined and their various strengths and weaknesses assessed, the three key concepts need to be tackled, namely 'cognitive', 'physiological' and 'emotional states'.

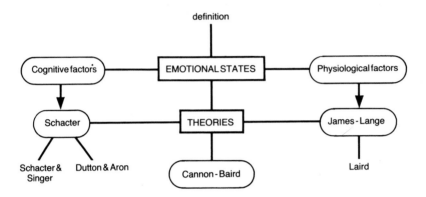

Emotion (from the Latin 'to stir up') is not easy to define. The physiological, cognitive and behavioural components should be mentioned, with each term clearly differentiated. Attempts to identify primary emotions (eg Ekman, 1972) could be referred to. The theories of James (1878) and separately of Lange, suggested that bodily changes preceed the interpretation of an emotion. Laird's (1974) work on the impact of facial expression, gives some support to this. However, Cannon offers detailed criticisms of the James-Lange theory, suggesting that physiological changes and subjective experience are *independent* of each other. The criticisms offered by Cannon should be supported with evidence. Finally, the cognitive labelling theory of Schacter can be presented. The classic Schacter and Singer experiment with adrenaline (1962) and the 'love on a high bridge' study by Dutton and Aron (1974), illustrate the importance of the interpretation given to physiological states, in defining the nature of the emotion experienced.

The diagrams that are sometimes used to illustrate these theories could be presented in a simplified form, *provided* the points they illustrate are made clear and discussed in the answer. There are many other studies that relate to these three main theories. These can be mentioned in greater or lesser detail, but should be integrated around the framework of the relative role of cognitive and physiological factors.

Discuss the view that intelligence is dependent on innate factors (1986)

What is meant by 'intelligence' may influence conclusions in this debate. Most studies to be quoted will be using IQ test results as synonymous with intelligence. A clear statement about the meaning of 'innate factors' should also be made. The implicit but missing aspect of the question – namely environment – needs to be mentioned, but is not initially the primary focus of the question.

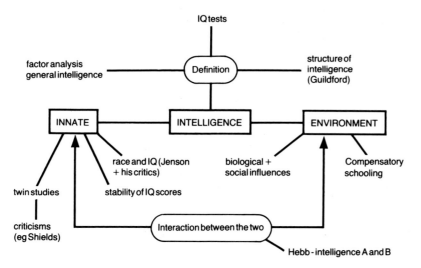

The evidence supporting the dependence on innate factors includes: (1) the role of genetic factors; (2) the stability of IQ scores over a lifetime. It is not necessary to get bogged down in detail on the many twin studies, but a selection of evidence quoting some correlation scores would help. Another line of argument is the highly controversial debate over race and intelligence. The predicted stability of IQ scores over a life-time is supported to a degree by longitudinal studies (eg Rubin and Balow, 1979, McCall, 1973). Yet even these studies suggest increasing variation in scores the longer the gap between measurements.

Further criticisms arise with studies that show the impact of environment on IQ scores (eg Skeels and Dye, 1939) and the success (itself debated) of educational interventions like 'Operation Headstart' in the USA. Hebb's (1949) argument about the necessary interplay between environment and heredity could form the kernal of a conclusion.

Discuss some of the criticisms that have been made of any ONE therapeutic approach

While one approach must be chosen, criticisms will often come implicitly or explicitly from others. The criticisms will generally address;

1 theoretical assumptions,

2 clinical practice,

3 success rates.

A clear, but brief, presentation of the approach is necessary, indicating its theoretical basis and the techniques used. Alternatives within the particular approach (eg Psychoanalysis and Client Centered therapy, or Cognitive therapy and Personal Construct therapy) could be brought out. Then the criticisms should be considered and backed with evidence.

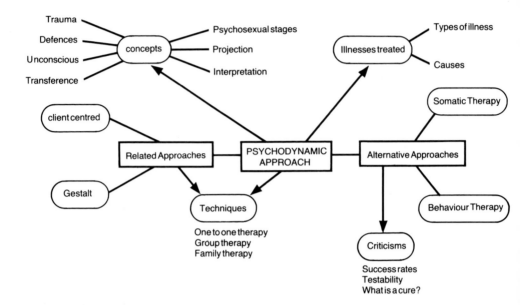

Using Psychodynamic therapy as an example, the Freudian assumptions should be outlined. The differences with, say, Jung and Erikson, could be mentioned. Related approaches would include both Carl Rogers' Client Centered therapy, and Fritz Perls' work with Gestalt. All use similar techniques. The key concepts underlying the Psychodynamic approach (especially trauma, repression and transference) should be looked at critically. They could be contrasted with the system related approach of Behavioural therapy. The issue of scientificity could be considered. The methods of treatment ie 'talking therapies', could be contrasted with the behavioural modification techniques and drug therapies. Much of this question revolves around what constitutes a 'cure'. The problem of defining mental illness and the relevance of the different approaches to neuroses, psychoses and personality disorders is raised in consequence. The claim by Eysenck that Psychoanalysis has a lower success rate (44%) than 'spontaneous remission' (66%) is countered by Bergin's more thorough survey (1971) and Smith (1980), who argue for a significant improvement in over 80% of the patients.

Examples of essays written under test conditions

In this next section we will look at specific examples of essays written in 45 minutes, under test conditions. They show what can be achieved for an examination. They are not all equally good, although they are all very competent answers. The first two are in answer to very similar questions on language and thought. They demonstrate that it is possible to answer questions in quite contrasting ways and that there is no one 'right' answer. Indeed it is worth repeating that this whole book is showing possible ways of approaching psychology questions and practicals. These ways are *not* the only ways.

'Language and Thought are intimately linked'. Discuss

There are many theories of how language and thought are linked (however all of them agree that both of these are dependent on the other). Thus we must say that they are intimately linked. However this is only with regards to their development. It is possible to think without speaking, similarly to speak without thinking, for example when you are reciting. However most of the time the two processes are linked.(1)

Primarily, we shall look at those psychologists who believe that thought is dependent on language, such as Whorf (1957). The Whorfian hypothesis, as it has come to be called, states that people who speak different languages perceive the world differently. This opinion was derived from studies on different Indian tribes. Whorf found that the Hopi Indians only had one word for aeroplane, insect or bird, whilst the eskimos had twenty words to describe snow. Also he found that the Hopi Indians classed orange, yellow and red under the same colour name. Thus Whorf argued they only perceived one colour.(2) Brown and Lennenberg (1954) disagreed with this. They compared English people's perception of colour with Shone and Bassai people. From this they concluded that the Shone and Bassai could perceive the different colours but because they did not have a name for the word they had trouble recognising it.(3)

Carmichael, Hogan and Walter (1957) also stated that factors other than language accounted for different perception. In their experiment they showed subjects a picture, for example:

One group was shown the label 'gun', whilst the other group was shown the word 'broom'.(4) The two groups were asked to

(1) This paragraph provides a general introduction, picking out the theme of interplay between the two concepts.

(2) The use of the word 'thus' here is misleading. The writer has not established Whorf's view as yet, and could make more of the fact that he considered that language determined perception and subsequent thought.

(3) The final sentence here is a little confused although the meaning is apparent.

(4) There are no marks going for illustrations, but a quick freehand sketch like this can be useful to make a point clear.

remember what they had seen. On retesting it was found that the label significantly altered the perception of the object. Carmichael suggested that this is the result of the memory not of the label.**(5)**

However, Carrol and Casagrande carried out an experiment that supported the Whorfian hypothesis. They studied three groups of children, Navaho, American white, and Navaho mixed with American white children. The hypothesis was that as the Navaho language stressed the importance of form the Navaho children should have better object recognition. This was found to be true. Whorf continued to say that the structure of language influences our perception of events. For example, in the Hopi language they would say the house flamed, not the house is on fire. Thus Whorf concluded the Hopi Indians must perceive the house as being the cause of the fire. Greene contradicted this by saying that too much emphasis was being placed on the language and that the Hopi Indians might find our habit of calling ships 'she' strange.**(6)**

Nowadays a weaker form of the hypothesis is accepted, that is language leads us to have different recognition levels of objects. There is another psychologist who believed that language was responsible for thought. Watson believed that thought was no more than electrical impulse created by the subtle movements made by our jaw bones. However Smith carried out an experiment wherein he was completely paralysed by a drug. After he regained normal movement he could tell others of the thoughts he had during the experiment, thus contradicting Watson. Now we shall look at another suggestion as to how thought and language are intimately linked.**(7)**

Piaget believed that thought was solely responsible for language and that language did not influence thought at all. He believed that the process between iconic and symbolic thought is natural and not due to the child's interaction with the environment.**(8)** Sinclair-De-Zwart supported Piaget in his two experiments in 1967 and 1969. Sinclair-De-Zwart concluded that a child could not grasp the essential meaning of words until it had developed the meaning of conservation.

Similarly Piaget is supported by observations on the deaf and blind. Furth (1966) found that deaf children did not develop language properly yet were not seriously delayed in developing the proper thought structures. Whilst Hatwell (1966) showed that whilst blind children could speak correctly, their thought processes were marred, thus thought is not reliant on language. Cromer (1973) criticised these studies as they had not looked at their subjects closely enough. In many ways this is true, the experiments supporting Piaget answer many questions, such as

(5) This could be explained a bit more clearly. Carmichael argued that the label might affect the memory rather than directly influencing the perception (which would be Whorf's position).

(6) This integration of arguments with subsequent criticism is useful. Greene is summarised very succinctly, but adequately.

(7) All the way through the writer seeks to link her paragraphs together. This achieves a coherence, and prevents the answer being just a list of studies.

(8) There appears to be some confusion here with Bruner's work.

how can a blind child develop meaningful language, but not meaningful thought?

It is here that we see the common sense of Bruner's ideas. Bruner was greatly influenced by Piaget and believed like Piaget that thought came first, in the iconic mode. However Bruner believed that language was vital for the development of thought from the iconic to the symbolic mode. Sonstreum (1960's) carried out an experiment to see whether Piaget or Bruner were correct. Sonstreum divided his subjects into four groups and studied their levels of conservation by allowing them to look at the remodelling of Plasticine in different ways. He found that only one group became significantly better at conservation and that was the group who spoke and played with the Plasticine at the same time. By making the child describe the Plasticine, Sonstreum stopped the child only noticing the shape, thus the child's thought was allowed to develop. Bruner's experiment had a similar result.**(9)** Piaget and Bruner both gradually developed their ideas until they agreed with those of Vygotsky.

Vygotsky believed that when people are born their language and thought are totally separate from each other. Language is meaningless and thought cannot be expressed. Around the age of two Vygotsky believed these two processes merged together, thus thought became rational, and language meaningful. Between the ages of two and seven these two processes became even more interlined with each other and thus inseparable. This is the opinion that is widely held today. However for a full complete view it is best to superimpose the ideas on top of one another.**(10)**

Diane Bowker

(9) It is not clear what experiment by Bruner is being referred to here. Nor is it clarified whether Sonstreum's experiment supported Piaget or supported Bruner.

(10) A concluding paragraph that quickly tied up the various strands of the argument would help.

This answer is impressive, both in terms of the amount of material that has been covered in 45 minutes, and the grasp of the argument. The *structure* is sound generally, although Carmichael could have been dealt with later in the essay, and his ideas related to the idea of language *influencing* thought. However, there are some loose ends in what is written. The *content* is more than adequate. Indeed, it might have been better to cut back a little on the content in order to make sure the steps of the argument were carefully demonstrated, especially in terms of a brief conclusion. The essay is written in a fluent *style* , and is generally easy to follow.

To what extent are thought and language related? (1985)

There are two theories put forward as to the relationship between thought and language: that of Piaget and Vygotsky who see thought as the primary function, and the Whorf-Sapir linguistic relativity theory where language is seen as the primary function.**(1)** Whorf-Sapir put forward a strong form; language determines thought; and a weak form; language can influence thought. There is no evidence to support the strong form but there is evidence for the weak form of their theory.**(2)**

Piaget says language is a tool which facilitates the thinking process and this would appear to hold true. Several studies have shown that thought goes on without language being readily available. Object permanence can be seen as the first sign of symbolic thought in a child at a time when it is unable to speak. In fact, when a child does learn to talk, it first utters one and two-word messages which convey a greater meaning than the words uttered.**(3)** This is evidence for a complex thinking process going on in the child's head. Telegraphic speech is the best example of information being organised into a minimal amount to convey maximum information. Evidence for thought without the need for language is shown by Firth 1966, who reports that deaf and mute non-signing adults score equally with 'normal' adults on IQ tests. This links to Bernstein's restricted and elaborated codes where working class children who use a restricted language score higher on non-verbal tests than on verbal. In this case their lack of higher vocabulary stunts their verbal performance but their performance on the non-verbal tests illustrates that they are of equal intelligence with children who score equally as well on verbal and non-verbal tests.**(4)**

Bernstein's (1976) research into the cognitive abilities of babies shows that babies can distinguish between focal colours without knowing their names. The babies register a different reaction to each colour suggesting that some thought process is being undertaken. The above research strongly contradicts the Whorf-Sapir strong linguistic relativity theory. If language determined thought then deaf-mute adults would have no IQ at all and babies would not be capable of any selective skills until they had learned the names of every object involved. Whorf-Sapir cite the Dani Indians who distinguish only between black and white, and the Zuni tribe who do not differentiate between orange and yellow as evidence for different world views coming about through different language. But, it is not that these tribes cannot see the differences in colours, they do not need to. Rosch (1973) and Brown and Lenneberg taught these tribes to make the differentiation which illustrates that they did not have isolated unchangeable world views.**(5)** So the relationship between thought and language is not a fixed, one way process, whereby a person's language means that they will think in a specific way.**(6)**

However, there is evidence to support language influencing thought, the weak form of linguistic relativity theory. In an ex-

(1) The essay commences in a way that is immediately relevant to the issue of the nature of the relationship between language and thought.

(2) This paragraph serves as a pointer for issues that are tackled more fully later in the essay.

(3) A brief mention of experimental evidence would back up this point, eg the studies made by Bower.

(4) This paragraph runs the risk of ranging over too wide a field, covering as it does, neonates, young children, telegraphic speech, deaf-mutes, and class related language codes. On the other hand it does highlight the variety of evidence that relates to this debate.

(5) The writer quite skilfully summarises the main points about a series of studies of tribes and colour perception. Her understanding of the arguments is demonstrated, without the specific details being presented at length.

(6) The final sentence of this paragraph makes a link back to the specific question.

periment by Carmichael, Hogan, Walters (1932) where verbal labels were given with ambiguous stimuli, the subjects tended to draw not what they had seen but what the verbal label had suggested. This suggests that our language influences how we store our concepts and how much attention is paid to unfamiliar items. In the Bartlett (1932) serial reproduction experiment Western subjects dropped the mystical, spiritual concepts from the story or changed them into 'westernised' concepts which they could understand and relate to better.**(7)**

From the evidence then it can be assumed that thought exists long before language is available and it is possible to think without having access to language. However, once language becomes a part of everyday functioning it can help to facilitate the thinking process. It can give definable terms to our thoughts and make them readily available. Language does, thus, influence thought because we tend to translate our ideas and thoughts into verbal descriptions, but thought will always be the primary function, after all, you can communicate without language but you cannot speak without thought.**(8)**

Jennifer Gunn

(7) These two studies are neatly juxtaposed – one showing the effect of language on concepts and the other, how concepts (relating to culture) influence language (ie memory for stories).

(8) The final paragraph makes a real attempt to conclude, coming down on the side of the primacy of thought in the relationship of thought and language.

This essay is particularly well *structured* , with a clear introduction, emphasising the main points of the debate, and a conclusion that follows on well from the evidence presented in the answer. The *content* is wide-ranging – almost too much so in places. Without one or two clear signposts, linking the material back to the question there would be the danger of the answer becoming confusing. However, the *style* is tight enough, and the expression of ideas sufficiently clear, to ensure that the answer remains relevant.

Discuss Psychological Investigations of Obedience and Conformity (1985)

There are several points to discuss when viewing the investigations concerning obedience and conformity. Do they prove what they set out to, and secondly what results do they obtain and are they relevant to society, an important point as conformity is a subject that deals with people's interactions with others.**(1)**

The main area of research into conformity is that of how the majority influences the minority. Through looking at two important experiments into this area we can see that the majority is a strong force whose powers are not be underestimated. In Asch's experiment (1952)**(2)** a subject seated second to last on a table, with approximately nine other subjects had to decide if a line S was the same length as any of three lines on another card, labelled A, B, C. It was found that whenever all the subjects, who were confederates, gave an obviously wrong answer

(1) The phrasing of this paragraph is poor but it provides a brief introduction, raising the issue of relevance.

(2) Asch's experiment is the 'classic' in this area. It is useful to give dates – especially for very significant studies, as this clarifies the order in which ideas developed in a given field. Sherif's much earlier (1935) experiment could have had brief mention.

before the actual subject's turn, thirty-three per cent of those subjects studied did not conform at all.**(3)** Crutchfield (1956) used a more economical approach as he tested all his subjects in five separate cubicles at the same time, by an intricate use of lights and panels. Crutchfield manipulated each subject into believing he was last. Again it was found that thirty per cent of the subjects conformed, in one case the subjects faced with a circle thirty per cent larger than a star, said that the star was larger because lights A-D had also said this.**(4)** These experiments explain many situations that occur in everyday life, such as a member of a gang who says he only committed a crime because the rest wished him to. However there is another area of research that at first appears to offer very contradictory evidence.**(5)**

This area of study looks at how the minority influences the majority. It seems unlikely that this would occur, but for such films as *Twelve Angry Men* to appear realistic it must happen. Schacter (1951) showed the effects of a minority on a group, but not how they influenced people. In his experiment on groups of approximately ten people, he introduced three confederates, a slider, a person whose opinion at first was different from the rest, but gradually he conformed, a mode, someone who agreed with the group from the start, and a deviant, someone who fervently disagreed with the group all along. Later on when questioned the deviant was seen as less attractive by the group members and over nominated for unattractive jobs. Thus it appears that to influence a group you had to be more moderate.**(6)** Moscovici in his experiment showed groups of subjects blue slides. A minority was seen to be more influential if they deviated by judging the slides greeny/blue, than if they deviated by calling them green. Contradictory to Schacter's results it was also found that to influence a group a subject had to be consistent – Nemeth. This shows how a minority can influence others. The Nazi party in the 1920s and early 1930s showed itself to be quite respectable with some right wing tendencies. Once it had gained support it did become more extreme, especially concerning the Jewish policies.**(7)**

Thus if a minority can influence a majority, we must look at why a minority conforms and obeys the majority in certain circumstances.**(8)** Overall the investigations showing who influences who can be explained in terms of situations. In Zimbardo's experiment, the reason why the prisoners became so subdued, and the quarrels so harsh, was partly accounted for by the point that they had created their own reality. Because the subjects were in a completely different situation they could make their own norms. Another explanation could be that as subjects are in an unknown situation, they look at others to see

(3) It is not necessary to learn endless statistics for these essays, but certain key findings – as with Asch – can be memorised to be used as illustrations.

(4) Note how briefly Crutchfield's quite complex experiment has been summarised.

(5) A clear link is made to the next idea to be dealt with.

(6) This Schacter example is an interesting illustration of group process and influence, but the writer does not make a clear connection to the concept of conformity.

(7) This is a useful illustration of the application of theory to specific events in society.

(8) Here the connection is made to the concept of obedience, using the idea of 'majority' and 'minority' – concepts which have been used to organise the essay as a whole.

how to behave – informational conformity. Schacter and Singer, showed that if a subject was injected with a drug epinephrine which they called suproxin, then put in a room with a confederate and if the subject was told that the drug had effects, they would be less likely to act like the confederate, than a subject who was not told. It was found that if the confederate acted euphoric or very angry, the subject, who had not been told, copied him.**(9)**

However there are other factors as well as situation that explain why we obey and conform. An investigation into the Jones Town massacre revealed that people had followed Jones' commands for two reasons. The first being the foot in the door technique theory. Jones only imposed a little on them at first, attending meetings, then gradually imposed on them more and more, until the people gave to Jones all their wealth and went to live in the temple. In everyday life this can be seen when a party candidate asks you to put a sticker on a window. If he has asked you to do this favour, you are more likely to put a poster up next time he asks. The second theory is self justification, people wished to justify to themselves why they were going to such meetings, so they entered into events with more vigour to justify what they were doing themselves. Milgram showed that people will do irrational things to obey a command. In his experiments he made subjects give electric shocks to people (who were actors, who had to pretend they were wired up) that were labelled severe shock. When questioned the subjects said that they would not have thought they would have. This explains why Jones followers were prepared to help him in his deceptions by going through people's rubbish, although they knew it was wrong.**(10)**

To conclude it appears that there are many theories of conformity that appear to conflict, but in reality only explain different aspects of one topic.

Diane Bowker

(9) An attempt is being made in this paragraph to explain *why* people obey. The illustration from Zimbardo's work is relevant. The Schacter and Singer study is also used to illustrate the point, but with less success, as the concepts of conformity and obedience are not really distinguished from each other.

(10) This paragraph covers a lot of ground – losing a little clarity on the way. It does avoid the trap of just retelling Milgram's experiment, and rather seeks to illustrate the concept of obedience using three different examples.

The *structure* of this essay is very clear, being built around the concepts of majority and minority influence. This enables a link to be made between the related but different ideas of conformity and obedience. There is sufficient *content* to illustrate the ideas being discussed, and the writer does not get lost in detail. The examples from history (the nazis and Jim Jones) are helpful. Overall the *style* is clear, although sometimes too many ideas are dealt with in one sentence, without their relevance being explained fully enough.

Discuss the factors involved in interpersonal attraction.

There is an old cliche which says that it is love which makes the world go round, however others beg to differ, such as Rubin

McNeil (1983) who believes that liking rather than loving is the more important. There are, however, certain determinants which make people like or love each other; some are characteristic to both, others are exclusive to one. These determinants are: physical attractiveness, similarity in attitudes, personality, reciprocity and proximity.**(1)**

(1) This paragraph provides quite a lively introduction ending with a list of issues to discuss.

However, there is one overall main theoretical approach to attraction which is called the social exchange theory introduced by Thibaut and Kelly in the late 1950s. They used a theory adapted from capitalist economics to explain friendship and love. They believed the following idea – we weigh up the costs and benefits of interacting with other people. The costs include such factors as embarrassment, anxiety and irritation. At the same time, dualistically, people are doing exactly the same to us. Thus, we barter our qualities and behaviour when choosing which people we wish to interact with, and are always trying to obtain the best 'deal' for ourselves. We weigh up our own past experiences and knowledge and observations of others we regard as similar to ourselves, what we can hope and expect to receive. Therefore if we find out that what – or rather who – we have is not up to our expectations, and we feel we are not getting what we deserve then we will find ourselves dissatisfied with the situation and start making attempts to look elsewhere. This theory is intended to apply at all levels, from looking for who to talk to at a party through to the extremes of looking for a husband or wife.**(2)**

(2) This is a good synopsis of social exchange theory, even if the phrasing gets a little bit obscure towards the end.

There is very little support for this theory, however, although Price and Vandenberg 1976 did find that the physical attractiveness of married couples in the USA correlated 0.30.**(3)** This shows a slight tendency for people to marry others who are similar to them in physical attractiveness although this is an extremely ambiguous and opinionated result.

(3) Relevant use of statistics, ie it is appropriate for the argument to be backed up occasionally by figures from research.

The other disadvantage to the theory is that although it is an attempt to explain behaviour it can in no way predict future behaviour. Thus the basic deduction of the theory is that people with 'similar' values will end up together. Thus people would have to be able to put a value on all the qualities about a person. This is surely a matter of opinion and not an entity which can be measured in a regular way.

To investigate friendships Mareno (1931) used sociometry – a method of studying group structures based on certain things and by collecting choices of the most or least preferred members of a group by each individual member. He found that the most popular people were those found to be the healthiest, wealthiest, most intelligent, attractive, sociable and helpful. Obviously there is a great flaw in the experiment and that is that it asks for ideal choices and does not take into account actual, real behaviour. Research into friendships has rested on the following factors; attitude, personality proximity and attractiveness.**(4)**

(4) A good link to the rest of the essay.

Firstly, attitudes. Bryne (1971) found that people were more likely to form friendships if they had similar attitudes. Arason and Worchel constructed questionnaires asking for responses from strangers who were either similar or dissimilar to the subjects in their attitudes. The subjects, however, were led to believe that the dissimilar strangers liked them, while the similar strangers disliked them. The subjects rated higher towards the dissimilar strangers who liked them and less to the similar strangers who they believed disliked them. Thus there is evidence here for reciprocal liking.

Newcombe investigated attitudes with previously unacquainted students who were housed together in groups of 17 for a period of a few months, during this time friendship patterns and attitudes were monitored. In the first experiment Newcombe found the friendships formed initially between room-mates, but later between people with similar attitudes to each other. He also saw people slightly change their own attitudes to match others in a better way. In his second experiment students were specifically selected to share a room with someone who was either similar or dissimilar to them. Unexpectedly the result was that all the room-mates stayed friends. This shows two things; firstly, that attitudes are important, but also secondly, that proximity is also important.

The second factor is personality.**(5)** Izard (1960) carried out an experiment whereby unacquainted female students were left to get to know each other. It was found that the three most liked and three least liked all had similar attitudes.

(5) Putting in markers like this keeps the factors being discussed clear.

The third factor is physical attractiveness. Adifoli (1975) found that the least liked group of students in a study when subjects were asked to choose a room-mate from their dormates were on average the most physically attractive. The most wanted and best liked group were those subjects who had previously scored highly on a personality test, but who were less attractive.

To conclude, it shows that no one factor causes friendship, but a mixture of many.

With regard to love, Rubin (1975) studied romantic attraction, and looked at the difference between liking and loving. Using a questionnaire he attempted to discover what the differences were. He concluded that in order to love someone there are certain characteristics which are exclusiveness, absorption, an obsessive want to help and dependency. In other words if you are in love with someone you will feel attracted to them by a powerful bond, you will be jealous of their relationships with others and would do almost anything for them.

Rubin tested his questionnaire by getting students to fill it in with their current dating partner in mind, and then a friend of the same sex. The questions on the love scale were like 'If I could never be with ———— I'd be miserable' and on the like scale they were like 'When I am with ———— we are always in the same mood.'**(6)**

(6) This is helpful detail.

Walster et al carried out an experiment in the 1960s where previously unacquainted students were given a dating partner for a dance. It was concluded that those partners who found each other physically attractive arranged another date, whilst those who did not made no other arrangements. However at a dance there is no chance for a person's personality to come through anyway.**(7)**

(7) Whether this is more to do with love, or should have been covered earlier in the essay when other studies of attractiveness were considered, is debatable.

Some psychologists believe that couples ought to have similar attitudes and needs, but Winch (1958) believed that couples ought to have complementary needs. For example, for one half to be dominant, the other to be submissive for a harmonious relationship to exist.

Apart from the above mentioned factors there are two other suggestions as to why people are attracted to each other.**(8)**

(8) While this forms a good link, it suggests that these are extra points that have just occurred to the writer. Perhaps no plan was made?

Firstly there is non-verbal communication suggested by Argyle (1975). He believed that attributes such as positive tone of voice and eye contact can make a person more attractive. It is highly believed that when a person is sexually aroused his or her pupils will dilate and this in turn has a favourable effect on the other person.

Secondly some people believed that pheromones are sexually attractive. These are the chemical odours given off by a person naturally from their day to day living. An experiment was carried out in a dentists waiting room and it was concluded that women sat nearer to a chair which had pheromones sprayed onto it.

Thus, there are evidently many factors which cause interpersonal attractions and it is also evident that it is not merely one of these factors which is outstandingly significant, but a mixture of all of them.

Georgina Meikle

While the essay is well supplied with sentences that guide the reader through, and link back to the question, the *structure* is a bit loose. Nevertheless, a wide range of studies is covered in a coherent way. The *content* is broad, and there is considerable detail in places. It is all relevant to the question. What is missing is an analysis at a more conceptual/theoretical level, to put the studies into a broader context. Generally, the *style* is clear with a good blend of illustration and explanation.

The Structured Question
and Statistics

In addition to standard essay questions, students are also confronted with questions on statistics and methodology. These are generally in a structured format, requiring a series of brief answers. The approach to questions like this is not the same as answering an essay question. Nor is it like filling out a questionnaire! The clue to tackling questions like this is to look at how they are formulated and what marks are being offered for the question. If there is only one mark going, then the answer almost certainly requires just one clear piece of information. For example:

Question
Define the term population as used in statistics (*1 mark*)

Answer
Population refers to a group of people or observations which includes all the possible members of that category.

A more elaborate question might carry three or more marks. This will require a fuller answer. The examiner will probably be looking for at least three distinct pieces of information, if three marks are on offer. It is helpful to include brief examples to back up any points that you are making to indicate that you have understood the question. For example:

Question
What is a repeated measures design and what are its advantages? (*3 marks*)

Answer
A repeated measures design is one way of approaching an experiment. In a repeated measures or within-groups design, the subjects undertake both the conditions of the experiment. For example, in an experiment on the Muller-Lyer illusion they may judge the length of the line in both the horizontal and the vertical condition. The main advantage of this design is that each subject acts as their own control. They are perfectly matched with themselves. Another advantage is that only half the number of subjects is needed compared to an independent measures design.

In this answer the term has been defined and a brief example given. Two advantages have been highlighted. The question does not ask for disadvantages, so these need not be given.

With structured questions, there is generally a stimulus passage describing an experiment. This should be read carefully, *at least twice* before you start answering the questions. Often the answers to at least some of the questions are contained directly in the passage. If they are not there directly, then there may well be a clue as to how to proceed.

There are two further parts of this book designed to help with questions of this type. The first is the section of questions which follow. These are designed to tackle most parts of an introductory syllabus on experimental methods. It is recommended that they should be answered prior to looking at the guidance on answers given at the end of the book. The final section of the book gives indications as to what could be included in answers rather than specific 'model answers'. The second is the section on statistics (pages 58–69). This is *not* intended to be a comprehensive text on statistics, but rather an introduction and an overview. It should be used in conjunction with one of the many excellent introductory texts on statistics that are available.

Statistics Questions

Statistics Question 1

You carry out a survey of 24 male and female students to see whether there is a sex difference in the perceptual set. You record the number who see the old lady as compared to the young lady, in the famous ambiguous picture used by Leeper (1935).

(a) What is the level of measurement of your data?

(b) You carry out a Chi^2 test on your data. What is meant by the *expected frequency* in this test? What number must the expected frequency equal or exceed, in order for the test to be valid?

(c) What are *degrees of freedom*? In this experiment, how many degrees of freedom are there?

(d) What is Yates' Correction correcting for, in this test?

(e) You find that your result is significant at $p \leqslant 0.05$ for a two tailed test. Explain what this statement means.

(f) This test is known as an inferential test. Explain the difference between inferential and descriptive statistics.

Statistics Question 2

In an experiment you are interested in the degree of relationship between scores on a test of mathematical ability and a test of verbal reasoning skills. Both are scored out of 100 and have proved to be reliable tests.

	verbal reasoning	mathematical ability
S_1	40	35
S_2	85	67
S_3	71	73
S_4	79	87
S_5	65	63
S_6	45	49
S_7	58	52
S_8	66	69
S_9	92	93

$N = 9$

(a) Explain the term *order effect*. In conducting this study, how would you control for order effect?

(b) Plot a scattergram for the scores. Does the scattergram indicate that a Pearson's Product Moment could be applied? Explain why/why not.

(c) What other conditions would have to be met for a parametric test to be carried out?

(d) A correlation of +0.91 was found on testing the results. This was significant for a one-tailed test at the 0.0005 level. What is the probability of making a Type I error in this experiment?

(e) Define a Type II error.

(f) To calculate the significance of a Pearson's Product Moment the value $N - 2$ is used. Another group of six students doing the same maths and verbal reasoning tests produced a correlation of +0.83. Using the simplified table below, state if this is significant, and to what level.

	Level of significance for a:		
	One-tailed test		
	0.05	0.025	0.005
	Two-tailed test		
$N - 2$	0.1	0.05	0.01
3	0.80	0.87	0.95
4	0.72	0.81	0.91
5	0.66	0.75	0.87
6	0.62	0.70	0.83
7	0.58	0.66	0.79

(After Clegg)

Statistics question 3

You undertake a test of memory with two groups. They are randomly assigned and you have 12 in one group and 13 in the other. In one condition the words are arranged in categories (eg animals, trees, colours etc). In the other, the words are presented in random order. You measure the number of words that are remembered after a one minute gap.

(a) What is the IV and the DV in this experiment?

(b) Suggest a suitable Null Hypothesis.

(c) Why is a Null Hypothesis used in an experiment?

(d) What type of design is used in this experiment?

(e) Define the following terms:
   Interval Data
   Ordinal Data

(f) You discover your results are non-parametric. What statistical test would you use to see if your results are significant?

Statistics question 4

Below is a sketch of a Normal Curve of Distribution. The positions of one and two standard deviations on each side of the mean have been drawn. The mean score is 80 and the standard deviation is 10.

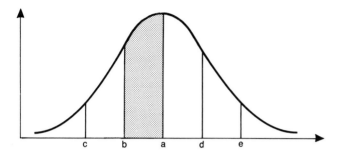

(a) What percentage of scores fall in the shaded area between a and b?

(b) Which line or lines represent the mean and the median?

(c) What is meant by the term *standard deviation*?

(d) What is the value or score represented at point e?

(e) If 2.3% of the scores are above point e, what is the probability of achieving a score of e or above?

Statistics question 5

You are interested in the effects of prolonged television viewing on aggressive behaviour and attitudes of school children. You randomly select a sample of 100 students, using the school roll, at an 11–16 school. You carry out various tests, and administer a questionnaire and an attitude inventory.

(a) What is your sampling frame?

(b) What is your overall population?

(c) Explain the value of having a random sample in this study. How might a random sample be selected from the school roll?

(d) Explain what is meant by *demand characteristics*. How might demand characteristics influence the way pupils respond to the attitude inventory?

(e) Suggest two ways in which you could assess the *reliability* of your attitude inventory.

(f) Define validity, and explain why a reliable test may not always be valid.

Statistics question 6

You are studying preferences for soap operas on TV. Your ten subjects rate two popular programmes on a scale from 1 to 7, where the higher the score, the more the programme is liked. You are unsure which, if any, will prove more popular. The results are as follows:

	Neighbours	Eastenders
S_1	1	4
S_2	3	7
S_3	3	5
S_4	4	5
S_5	4	2
S_6	3	4
S_7	1	6
S_8	2	6
S_9	3	6
S_{10}	7	6

(a) What type of design has been used in this experiment?

(b) What level of measurement is achieved with this data?

(c) Suggest an experimental hypothesis for this study. State if it is one or two tailed.

(d) A Wilcoxon Test is carried out, and Wilcoxon's T statistic = 7. This proves to be significant at the 0.05 level for a two-tailed test. Would it be more significant for a one tailed test?

For guidance on how to answer these questions refer to pages 104–106

Planning a Practical

The careful planning of a practical can save a lot of heartache later. There are various stages in designing a practical.

1 Selecting a suitable problem to study.
2 Making sure that you have sufficient background material on the area you are interested in.
3 Deciding on a suitable design.
4 Developing the appropriate apparatus.
5 Clarifying the nature of the data you will collect and a suitable statistics test.

If each of these stages is carefully accomplished, then the practical can be successfully undertaken. Also, the writing of the report will not prove to be too burdensome. If you are following a course that requires a number of practicals to be completed, then it is as well to ensure that you choose ones with sufficient variety. This will ensure that you experience different techniques first hand and also that you practise a variety of statistical procedures.

We will now consider the steps in planning a practical in more detail. Students will find it helpful to write out brief responses to each of these steps *prior* to undertaking the practical. This will ensure that what they are going to do is feasible and can be accomplished.

Selecting a suitable problem to study

It is helpful while you are following a course in Psychology, to keep one page at the back of your file for jotting down ideas that occur for practical work. Often something that you read, or an idea mentioned in a lecture or class discussion can form the basis of a worthwhile investigation. If you are stuck, then thumbing through one or two good textbooks will provide a variety of ideas. You do not need to choose the exotic. A simple idea investigated appropriately and accurately, is quite sufficient. Often it is quite acceptable to just replicate an idea that has been already tested. You may wish to add refinements or to develop your own ways of measuring the variables involved.

You need to ensure that there is sufficient background material on the topic that you are interested in to allow you to write your report. Particularly, when you are clear about what your independent variables are, you need to check that there is some background discussion that you can draw on which relates to those variables. For example, if gender is your independent variable in an experiment on memory, then you need to establish if there are any theoretical discussions or empirical studies that relate gender as such, to the specific aspect of memory you are considering. Judicious use of the indexes of text books, as well as careful searching of the library stacks is important at this stage.

Developing a Working Hypothesis

During the planning stage you may not be able to precisely formulate the hypothesis that you wish to test. Nevertheless, at this stage it is most helpful to have a rough conjecture about what it is that you are investigating. When you have clarified what you are going to do, by reading and discussion, then you can formulate your hypotheses in a more scientific form. At this stage you need an idea to guide your planning.

Formulating the Independent and Dependent Variables

It is vital that you are clear about what your variables are. Even for an observation or a correlation, you need to be clear on this point. In common parlance, you are deciding what is doing what to what. You are establishing what you think may be the causal links or associations in what you are investigating. Write them down. Then check that you have clearly specified what is manipulated in the independent variable and how change will be measured in the dependent variable. For a correlation or observation, be clear about how you will measure or record the changes or effects you are interested in.

Type of design and sample

Specify what type of design you are going to use. How many groups will you be investigating? Will the design be repeated measures, matched groups or independent measures? How will you choose your sample? How will they be allocated? If it is matched groups, what will be the criteria by which you will match your subjects?

You need to decide on your sample size and their composition – in terms of age, class, sex, educational background and so on.

Controls

What controls will be necessary? Will you need to counterbalance to control for order effect? How will you ensure there is no experimenter effect – or operation of demand characteristics (where the subjects do what they think you want them to do). How will you control for extraneous variables? Where will you do your study and when?

Apparatus

This is where you *operationalise* your study. You need to design any apparatus that you are going to use. This will be particularly important if you are designing an attitude scale or a simple personality inventory. Even if you are using apparatus from some other source, you will need to check that it is appropriate to your needs.

Pilot study

In some instances, it will be advisable to carry out a brief pilot study to ensure that the apparatus you are going to use is appropriate, and that it works. In the light of this any necessary adjustments can be made.

Type of data expected

You should establish what sort of data your study will be likely to produce.

Type of statistical test to be used

In relation to the design you have chosen, and the data you expect to gather, you can decide what statistical tests are likely to be most appropriate. This will allow you to be sure that you do a spread of tests, and to avoid finding each experiment you do leads to the same statistical test.

Level of significance chosen

Another decision you need to make, is about the level of significance that will be appropriate for your study. Generally a probability level of 0.05 will indicate that there is an effect taking place. If it is important to avoid a Type I error, however, then a lower level of probability should be chosen – say 0.025 or 0.01.

Types of Practical

The most usual type of practical undertaken is the experiment. However, there are three other types of practical which we can consider, namely the observation, the correlation and the case study. We will consider each in turn.

The experiment

The experiment follows the traditional scientific model. In a study of this sort a specific hypothesis is being tested about the causal effect of a particular variable. For example, it might be predicted that a noisy environment would have an impact on the performance of a mathematical test. The alternate or experimental hypothesis might be 'that the scores on a mathematical test will be significantly higher when it is taken in a quiet environment, than when taken in a noisy environment'. The independent variable (IV) would be the type of environment and the dependent variable (DV) would be the scores achieved on the maths test. This is therefore a test of difference – that is the effect that *different* values or conditions of the IV will have on the DV. Strictly, in an experiment, it is the null hypothesis that is being tested. This would state that 'there will be no significant difference between the scores obtained for the maths test in the noisy environment or in the quiet environment.' The null hypothesis is falsifiable. If it is proved wrong in the experiment, then it is possible to *support* the experimental hypothesis (note: we do not say *prove*).

In an experiment the investigator is seeking to establish the *causal link* between the two variables being investigated. Hence this type of design is known as a causal design. A causal design requires that the independent variable can be manipulated. This condition does not really apply to a correlation.

Correlation and other non-causal designs

A correlation or test of association looks at the relationship between variables. Here the interest is in how the change in one variable is associated with the change in another variable. If we wished to establish whether there was a possible link between lead pollution and intelligence, we might measure the distance children live from a major road and see if it correlated with their intelligence as measured by an IQ test. We might be interested to test out Rokeach's idea of dogmatism and prejudice. Here we would look at people's score on a dogmatism scale and see how it related to their score on a measure of racism and sexism. We would need, in each case, to control for other possible variables that might influence the outcome. In the first, the income of the parents and how long the child had lived in their house would be among the most relevant. In the second, educational level or intelligence might be important variables to control for. In both cases – and indeed with all correlations – we cannot assume that an association means a causal link.

It is because correlations are not causal designs that we cannot really talk about an IV and a DV in this context. The two variables may not be related at all. For example, there is probably a positive correlation between the age of marriage and the sale of pop records. Both may well have risen over the last ten years. However, we cannot assume any necessary relationship (although there may be a loose link) in terms of changes in the economy.

When designing a correlational study (and writing about it) it is important to specify what the variables are that are being studied. Also, it may be that you will assume the possibility that one is more fundamental (causal) than the other. This can be treated as approximating an IV. However, you need to bear in mind that neither a positive nor a negative correlation demonstrates a causal link.

There are other experimental designs which are also, strictly, non-causal. They do not really constitute correlations either as they are tests of difference. These non-causal designs occur when the IV cannot really be manipulated. An example of this is a comparison of males and females for a given psychological characteristic. For example, if we compared the skill of males and females on a manual dexterity test, we do not manipulate the sex as a variable, we just use an independent-measures design. We cannot say that sex differences *cause* differences in manual dexterity. It may well be some other factor altogether, like socialisation. Because no direct cause can be assumed, this type of design is also non-causal. However, in all other respects it can be treated as an experiment.

Non-Experimental Methods and Observational Studies

Non-experimental methods would include observations, surveys and case studies. Students may well wish to experience one or more of these first hand, as the approaches differ in a number of respects from an experiment.

Survey

This is used where direct observation is not possible. Kinsey's famous survey of sexual behaviour and the Newson and Newson study of child rearing approaches are two prominent examples of this technique. The careful selection of a suitable sample, and the administration of interviews or questionnaires, are the main techniques involved here. Attitude surveys, adapted or developed by students, can provide interesting and challenging practical work.

The case study

Freud made particular use of this approach. His in-depth description of the psychological functioning of 'The Wolf Man' is a particularly striking example. This analysis, completed in 1915, delved into the biography and childhood experiences and relationships of one man. It sought to explain his adult manic-depression, in terms of various childhood neuroses. In the case study then, the focus shifts to the individual. It is an *idiographic* approach: in other words it is a qualitative description of individual factors influencing behaviour. It tends to concentrate on what is unique in the experience of one person.

Another example is provided by the highly readable study of *Sybil* by Schreiber (1973). This describes the possible causes of multiple personality in a young woman. Again the current behaviour and therapeutic treatment is explored in terms of childhood trauma.

A case study is not an easy form of study to accomplish successfully by students. If it is undertaken, considerable thought should be given to what the form of the study will be, and how evidence will be recorded. Without a clear direction a case study can just end up as a diffuse description.

The observation

This is an important psychological technique, which differs substantially from the laboratory based experiment. The work of ethologists like Lorenz and Tinbergen have demonstrated the value of this approach in relation to studies of animals. Festinger (1956), who joined a sect that believed the world was imminently due to end, showed how useful such in depth study would be. His theory of cognitive dissonance developed, in part, out of that study to explain the response of the cult members when the world did not end.

Festinger's work can be described as *participant observation*, because he participated covertly as a sect member. Many observation studies may be covert, in so far as those observed are not aware they are being studied, but students are less likely to be involved in full-blown participant observation studies. It will be helpful to look in some detail at the methods and techniques involved in observational studies.

Observation – some basic techniques

Observations require careful planning. Anyone in doubt on this point should choose any social situation and try 'just observing' for a few minutes. The vast variety of things occurring means that what is observed has to be a selection. Any two people just observing the same scene, will actually 'see' different things.

The observation needs to be structured and organised in terms of a specific problem or hypothesis. Indeed some observations can be considered as 'natural experiments'. These we will consider first.

Natural experiments

In a natural experiment you will choose some naturally varying condition (eg full underground carriages or nearly empty ones) and observe some effect (eg non-verbal communication, body posture etc). Alternatively, you may introduce a variable by getting a fellow experimenter to sit at varying distances from people on benches in public parks or shopping centres. Their behaviour can then be observed. In a natural experiment the subject does not know they are part of an experiment. As a technique, it is a sort of half-way house between an experiment and an observation.

Organising and recording data

As observations are so open-ended, a way of organising data is imperative. The data need to be recorded in a systematic fashion. For example, if you were going to investigate the fixed action patterns of a rat, you might record the rat's behaviour every five seconds, on some sort of check list. In this way you would have a record both of the frequency of types of behaviour, and their sequence.

Certain techniques that help with organising data are;

event sampling
time sampling
rating scales

1 Event sampling
   This is where every time a particular behaviour occurs it is recorded. In order to do this a list of possible behaviours needs to be drawn up first. Then a check or tick can be made on each occasion a specific behaviour is undertaken.

2 Time sampling
   Again this requires a check list. As in the fixed action patterns example given above, the predominant behaviour in any given time period is recorded. This can be used for observing single subjects or groups.

3 Rating scales
   For given types of behaviour a series of scales is developed. Then the observer will complete these scales for individuals or groups. For example, if observing a group of children, scales might be produced for aggressive behaviour, co-operative activity, degree to which they ask for help, initiate activity, talk and so on. The scale could be five or seven check points, with guidance like 'always talking, talks sometimes, seldom talks'. At the end there will be a profile for each participant for each of these characteristics.

Other techniques could involve the following:

1 Using a video camera
   This can be particularly effective for recording group interactions. It means that behaviour can be analysed carefully after the event.

However, the video itself is too 'raw' as it stands and the data in it may need to be organised, using one of the methods already discussed.

2 Using a camera
This can catch key moments in a behavioural sequence. It is a technique that can be used to back up other forms of observation.

3 Using a tape recorder
This could be used to monitor behaviour, eg the questions a teacher directs to boys as compared to girls in a class. An accurate record like this allows precise analysis of language used. Also small portable tape recorders could be used to allow verbal descriptions of behaviour as the observation takes place. They will be a bit like a sports commentary. The problem with this method is that the material will have to be transcribed later, which is a time-consuming process.

4 Making sketches
Swift diagrams or sketches are another method by which observations can be captured. These could be done, for example, for a time sample of where children are in a room relating to various toys or stimuli.

When data have been collected, they need to be effectively presented. Often descriptive statistics can be used – for example histograms or pie charts. If the observation has involved cameras, tape recorders, or written or sketched accounts, then quotations, extracts or summaries of these can be effectively used. The important consideration here is that a careful distinction must be made between what has been actually observed and the interpretations of the observer. As Stern (1930) argued, in considering observations of children, no conclusions should be drawn which cannot be positively justified by the actual observation.

Experiments in Psychology

The following pages give brief outlines of a number of possible practicals. They have been deliberately left a little open ended, so that the construction of suitable hypotheses and the development of a full procedure will need to be worked out by the student. Each of the suggestions has been tried successfully by students.

The first examples are of observation studies on children. These are covered in some detail, and should be read in conjunction with the section on observation (see pages 47–50).

Studying children: use of observation

It is a very enjoyable function of a course in Psychology, to spend some time doing a study on an aspect of developmental psychology. This is often an excellent opportunity to undertake an observation. A letter or a personal approach to a play group or primary school will usually result in permission being granted, if you have a clear idea of what it is you want to study, and how you will go about it.

It is possible to undertake an experimental design, and to test out, for example, some of Piaget's experiments, and those of his critics (see pages 9–14). The design will usually be independent measures, comparing different age groups. However, we will consider an observational study. You need to decide which aspect of the children's behaviour you wish to observe. Two examples will be considered here. The first will investigate types of play. The second will focus on interaction patterns in groups.

1 Children's play

You will need to take a theory about children's play, and decide which aspect you wish to investigate. This will be influenced by the children you have access to, their ages, and the situation in which you will be observing them. A preliminary visit to your school or group is therefore very important.

You might wish to focus on the difference between ordinary play and challenging play (see Sylva and Lundt, *Child Development: a First Course* 1982 pps. 164–170). In challenging play the activities are more demanding, whereas ordinary play is simpler, requiring fewer skills and less use of the imagination.

Apparatus

The important factor in a naturalistic observation is the observation schedule. This is a record of the activities that you observe. It allows behaviour to be classified and recorded against time. In the diagram the type of schedule used by Sylva *et al* in their observation study is given. Such a schedule allows quick notes to be made, while observing, and for a pattern of behaviour to be built up over time. Each column needs only to have brief notes, minute by minute. For example under 'Social Setting' might go 'solitary', 'child pair' 'small group', 'large group'. With 'play' a few categories would be developed from your initial observations (eg 'pretend play', 'small scale construction' etc). With 'language', codes could be used to indicate the target child (TC) another child (OC) or an adult (A).

Minute	Activity	Language used	Social setting	Play theme

(Adapted from Sylva and Lundt)

Procedure

You still need to give thought to your design, in the sense that you may wish to compare different naturalistic settings. The variables you might deal with could include age, free play *vs* organised play, sex of children playing, types of toys available, time of day etc.

The schedule you use should be tested out and adapted if necessary. You could back it up with use of other recording devices eg a tape recorder, camera or video. It is best if the children can get used to your presence a bit before you start your observation or you may become the key variable determining their behaviour.

Results and statistics

The results for an observation differ from those of an experiment, for you are unlikely to use inferential statistics. You may use some descriptive statistics, but generally your findings will be composed of verbal descriptions. These should be organised to illustrate the particular aspect of the children's activity you were investigating. If it is a contrast between simple and complex play, then various short descriptive passages could provide 'pen sketches' of the points you wish to illustrate.

By all means include diagrams, photos, brief transcriptions from tape or video, but make sure that what you include is demonstrably relevant to the theme of your study.

2 *Leadership in children's groups*

A more formal study using older children could use Bales' schedule of leadership behaviour in groups, or any other suitable classificatory scheme. Bales' scheme is based on analysing people's behaviour in terms of the emotional area and the task area. The emotional area is analysed in terms of positive and negative reactions. The task area is scored in terms of asking questions and attempting answers. Such a study would benefit from the use of a video camera, to allow for a more detailed analysis of interactions but this is not vital, especially if the observation is being carried out by a team. The group or groups of children will need to be given a suitable discussion topic or problem to solve.

Apparatus

Again, an observation schedule needs to be devised which focuses on the issues of interest eg leadership behaviour. A video camera which can record the whole group, with chairs suitably arranged (eg in a crescent shape), will be valuable. Alternatively, a tape recorder could be used, but it may prove difficult to be sure who is speaking.

Procedure

Time needs to be given to allow the group to settle down before starting the observation. The children will need to be very clear about the problem they are to discuss, how long they have to come to a decision, and any other 'ground rules' they need to be told about. Make sure you check that your video/tape recorder is actually recording. Nothing is more frustrating than completing your observations only to find the microphone was not switched on!

Results and statistics

As with the previous observation study, these will need to be tailored to the specific issue you are investigating. If you have compared groups, you may wish to present your results showing;
a) the similarities between each group,
b) the differences that occur.
Use of suitable quotes, diagrams and descriptions should illustrate the points you wish to make, relating to the basic hypotheses you are investigating.

Investigating Perceptual Set

In designing an experiment it is not necessary to go for great complexity in order to achieve a result. Simple apparatus will often be sufficient. The following experiment requires eight small squares of card and a stop clock. It is designed to test the proposition that subjects will tend to be reluctant to see or recognise a word that is considered rude. The background to this idea covers psychoanalytic concepts of defence and repression, social psychological ideas on conformity, behaviourist theories on reward and punishment, as well as the various arguments concerning perceptual set.

Apparatus*

Eight small squares of card. On four the word *HITS* is written. On the other four is the word *SHIT* (other similar words could be used). The letters overlap more than one card, so that on any one card will be the part of a letter or the parts of two. The cards are made so that only

(* idea developed by Diane Bowker)

one of the two words can be constructed, in each case. In addition to this a stop watch is required and a pen and paper to record the results.

Procedure

The design will be independent measures. Subjects will be asked to arrange the four cards, presented face down, into a word. They will be told to start, and will be timed from that point onwards. The timing will stop when the word is arranged in front of them with the four cards touching each other.

Statistics

An independent t-test is likely to be appropriate, as the data will be interval. It will have to be checked to ensure it is parametric.

Sight, sound and dexterity

A very simple design can be used to test the proposition that the presence of sound influences motivation and skill in playing video games. This experiment would touch on perception, physiological psychology, motivation and possibly learning theory.

Apparatus

You will need access to a computer and a suitable computer game or two – where sound is used. With a suitable room, a stop clock and pencil and paper to record results, you will be under way.

Procedure

You need to take care over your design. You will have to *counterbalance* in order to control for *order effect*, if you use a repeated measures design. This is preferable as the variation in experience and skill, with computer games is considerable. A matched subjects design or independent measures design could be used, but would probably need to involve considerably more subjects.

A trial run will be valuable to ensure that your instructions are clear

and that the games are neither so easy that you get a '*floor effect*', nor
so difficult that you have a '*ceiling effect*' in your measurements.

One other problem will be subjects guessing what the experiment is
about and so producing a self-fulfilling prophecy (or an experiment
with '*demand characteristics*' (see page 106). You will need an explanation with modest subterfuge!

Results

The results will be scores that will probably achieve interval status.
You will need to check if your overall data are parametric. Then, depending on your design, you will need a suitable test of difference.

Selective attention and personal stereos

The availability of stereo tape recorders, and the portability of personal
stereos, means that it is possible to replicate a number of the classic
studies of selective attention, testing the theories of Broadbent, Treis-
man, Deutsch and Deutsch, and Norman. Although the theories differ,
the apparatus remains much the same.

Apparatus

You will need to, either obtain a stereo recording system on which you
can record separate messages on the two different stereo channels, or
to use two portable stereos. In the second case one stereo carries one
message and the other the second. You will have to use some ingenuity
with the headphones to ensure the correct message goes to the appropriate ear. This experiment stands or falls on the choice of material
that you record and the quality of the recording, so care should be
taken over this.

Procedure

This is another instance where a careful pilot study is essential, firstly
to make sure that you are confident with the apparatus, and second to
test that it works in the way that you expect it will. Your design will
probably be independent measures, as you are likely to want to use the
same stimulus materials, but require the groups of subjects to do different things with it. As subjects can be a bit embarrassed doing
'shadowing task' (where they say aloud what they hear in one ear),
you may need to take time putting them at their ease, and choosing a
suitable place to carry out the experiment.

Results

The data you obtain may be of interval status, you will need to decide
if they really are more than just ordinal. If your design is independent
measures then your choice will be between an independent t-test (if the
data are parametric) or a Mann-Whitney.

Your results would include examples of the sort of errors made in
the shadowing tasks, if these appear to be relevant to the hypothesis
that you are testing.

Embedded Figures Test

In perceiving the world about us, we continually separate out background from the object in the foreground. When we see a bus coming down a road, we perceive the bus distinctly from the features which surround it. The ability to separate out simple figures within a more complex design, appears to be related to other aspects of an individual's psychology. This can be tested. The apparatus developed by Witkin *et al*, uses a series of cards with complicated diagrams, and other cards with simple diagrams. The subject is required to find the simple figure within the complex one. The length of time taken, over a series of cards, gives a score. This represents their degree of field-dependence or independence. This can be considered as a scale between two extremes.

Witkin found that the capacity to separate the *figure* from the *ground* appeared to correlate with the way the subject thought, or their 'cognitive style'. This he described in terms of two 'polar opposites', the *global* and the *articulated*. There is not space here to go into the details of this classification. He discovered that this capacity to separate figure from ground was associated with a range of other ways of thinking. These include:

The body image The degree to which the body is experienced as having definite limits and being made up of discrete/separate parts. This can be assessed through drawings.

Forming opinions The degree to which a subject will be influenced in their opinions, by the presentation of an authoritative source, giving a particular opinion eg an article in a paper.

Also, sex/gender differences have been found.

Apparatus

It is possible to construct a simple version of this experiment, by using a range of figures that are given in some text books. An example of the type of drawing that could be used is shown here:

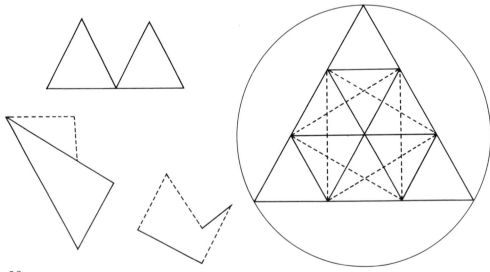

A student could draw their own, or obtain pictures with hidden figures from children's books/comics.

In addition to a picture, a stop watch will be necessary.

Further apparatus will be determined according to which factors the experimenter wishes to correlate with the degree of field-dependence.

Procedure

Using whatever apparatus has been chosen, the subjects are invited to find the hidden figures in the picture(s). The speed with which all/most of the pictures can be found will give a measure of the degree of field-independence. This will then be followed (with due controls for order effect) by a suitable measure for whatever other aspect of thinking style is to be studied.

Statistics

The data may be parametric, in which case a Pearson's Product Moment may be appropriate, if the data approximate to a straight line. If a comparison is being made of gender differences, then an independent t-test may be used.

Simple Guide to Statistics

In order to successfully plan your practical work and effectively design an experiment, you need to be aware of the statistical procedures you will be using. To aid this the next section provides an overview of basic statistics, relevant to psychology. As stated previously in this book, this section is not intended to be a mini text on statistics, nor is it adequate on its own, to cover the needs of a student pursuing an examination course. However, it is intended as a succinct introduction to the main concepts that students are likely to come across. In particular it will form a useful reference in planning an experiment, especially with regard to choosing the correct statistical test for the experimental report. At the revision stage, it can be used along with the questions given earlier, as a checklist of major terms and concepts that must be understood to successfully negotiate the examination.

The aspects covered in this section are:

descriptive and inferential statistics

probability and types of error

experimental design

data and levels of measurement

the normal curve of distribution

parametric and non-parametric tests

robustness and sensitivity of tests

choosing statistical tests

Descriptive statistics

Any psychological investigation will produce data of some kind. If these can be represented in some numerical form, then descriptive statistics can be used. Descriptive statistics, as their name suggests, just describe the basic findings. When the weatherman on TV gives the day's sunshine totals, these are descriptive statistics. Similarly, when a researcher gives the results of an IQ test, he or she is using descriptive statistics.

For our purposes, we can consider the presentations of selected data in the form of bar charts, pie charts, graphs and tables to be one type of descriptive statistic. More usually the term is applied to two aspects of the figures. The first is concerned with a number that most completely represents the whole lot (the central tendency). The second measures the spread or variability of the scores (the measure of dispersion).

The central tendency

We will consider three measures of central tendency. The first is probably the most useful, and should be given, where appropriate, in most reports. It is the mean.

> The mean of a set of numbers or scores is the sum of all the scores divided by number of scores in the set.

The second measure of central tendency is the median. This, as its name suggests, is the number which has as many numbers above it as below it, when the numbers have been put in rank order.

> The median is the value of the central score in a distribution of scores arranged in rank order.

Where two scores occupy this central position then the average of the two is taken.

The third measure is the mode. This is the actual score which occurs most often in a group of scores.

> The mode is the most frequently occurring score in a given distribution of scores.

It is possible to have two or more modes where there are a number of different scores all occurring with equal and greatest frequency.

Measure of Dispersion

A set of results or scores does not only have a central tendency, but also a degree or amount by which they are spread out. This is the amount of variability in the scores. One way of indicating the dispersion is to consider the range.

> The range is the difference between the smallest and largest scores in a distribution.

This is a rough and ready measure because it ignores all the data between the two end scores. A more sensitive measure is called the variance. This is closely related to a statistic that is central to many tests, the standard deviation. What these two statistics do is provide a number or value, which represents the spread of all the scores around the mean.

The variance and the standard deviation are measures of the dispersion of a set of scores or their variability around the mean. The variance is calculated by finding the difference of each score from the mean. The sum of the square of each of these scores is found, and divided by the total number of scores. The standard deviation is the square root of the variance.

Variance In the cartoons there are two groups of people waiting at bus stops. If we were to measure their heights and find the average, we might discover that the *mean* height was exactly the same for both. This descriptive statistic is, therefore, not enough to adequately describe these two samples. We need a statistic that will pick out their differences. This is the *variance*. With this measure, the differences in height of the circus group will show up in contrast to the similarity in height of the ballerinas.

Inferential statistics

Returning to our earlier example, the weatherman not only describes the past day's weather, but also predicts the future weather. Such a prediction is inferential. To take another instance, if an IQ test has been conducted on a random sample of students in a particular college, then it may be possible to infer from the results something about the IQ of all the students in the college. The statistical tests which you use in psychology are designed to see if the independent variable has had an effect on the dependent variable. When using statistical tests we see to what extent we can infer that any difference or change in scores can be attributed to the independent variable rather than to chance factors.

> Independent variable (IV) – This is the variable that is expected to produce a change in another variable. By manipulating this variable the experimenter sees if a change is produced in the dependent variable.

For example, in an experiment on memory, the independent variable may be whether the group has been advised to make mental images of words given in a list or not. The dependent variable is then the number of words remembered under the two conditions. Statistics can be used to see if it is possible to infer whether any differences in the two scores can be explained by the effect of the IV rather than chance.

> Dependent Variable (DV) – This is the variable that is affected, or may be affected, by the IV.

Probability and Types of Error

When you throw a dice, there is a one in six chance that you will throw a six. If you want a six, and you do throw a six, then this is hardly significant. If you were to do it three times in a row, and you were claiming extra-sensory powers, then it would appear more significant. The probability of three sixes being thrown by chance is slight. However, it must be remembered that there is 1 in 216 ($6 \times 6 \times 6$) chance that it would happen by chance. With inferential statistics you are computing the likelihood that your result has occurred because of the effect of the independent variable. It must always be remembered that the possibility exists that the result, however impressive, may have occurred by chance, (or for reasons other than the IV eg the dice has a magnet inserted under one of its faces!).

Generally, psychologists accept that the IV does appear to be having an effect on the DV when the likelihood of the event occurring by chance is down to 1 in 20. This is 5 times in 100 and is expressed as a probability level of $p \leq 0.05$. A more rigorous standard to make sure the IV really is likely to be producing an effect, would be obtained by choosing a lower probability level (eg $p \leq 0.01$). (NB $\leq$ means 'less than or equal to'.)

Raising the probability increases the likelihood the result has occurred by chance.	Lowering the probability decreases the likelihood the result has occurred by chance.
This can lead to a *Type 1 Error* where we decide the IV has had an effect on the DV when it has not.	This can lead to a *Type 2 Error* where we consider the IV has had no effect on the DV when it has.

Design

Imagine an experiment where the effect of noise levels on a maths test was being investigated. Here the IV, noise level, can be directly manipulated. With careful control, the effect of this manipulation on the DV, performance in the test, can be measured. Here the change in the IV is apparently the direct cause of the change in the DV. The design is causal.

In another experiment, the performance of females on a perception task is compared with that of males. The IV here is gender. However, we cannot be sure that any measured differences on the perception task between the two groups were caused by biological differences. The cause might be some other factor, like socialisation. Strictly, we have to say that the experimenter cannot directly manipulate the IV and so the design is really non-causal.

Both of these designs are tests of differences between groups or conditions. We are looking at how a change in conditions produces a change in some other factor. There are three fundamental designs; repeated measures, matched groups and independent measures.

Repeated measures   If an experiment uses the *same* group of subjects under different conditions, then this is an example of a *repeated measures* design. With this type of design, each subject acts as their own control because any extraneous variables, like how tired they are, what they have eaten, their physical or mental skills etc. can be expected to be the same under both conditions.

Repeated measures: here one group carries out the same task under two different conditions. This can also be called within-groups related design.

Matched groups: here two groups are matched as carefully as possible in pairs. They are allocated randomly to one or other groups. Each group carries out the task under a different condition of the IV. This can also be called a matched-pairs related design.

Independent measures: here subjects are randomly allocated to one of two groups. This can also be called a between groups unrelated design.

Matched groups   Where a repeated measures design is not possible, because performing under one condition of the IV would influence performance under the other condition (e.g. in a problem solving experiment, where a clue is given), a *matched pairs* design may be used. Here subjects are matched in pairs that are as similar as possible for all relevant characteristics. They are then each allocated to different groups. The groups can then be treated as though they were repeated measures, for statistical purposes.

There is another type of non-causal design. This is the correlation, where the degree of relationship or association between two characteristics, is being measured. Often a correlation will assess the degree

63

of association of two characteristics in the same individuals. For example, rating people for introversion-extroversion and also for prejudice.

Correlational designs usually use 'repeated-measures' in terms of the way they are conducted. Sometimes they will require matching groups. However, it must be remembered they are not testing for differences but for relationships, and they are not causal.

Independent measures   It is difficult and time consuming to try and set up an experiment with matched groups, and not all experiments can be repeated measures. Many use two groups, not necessarily of equal numbers, who experience the different conditions of the experiment. This type of design is *independent measures*. Allocation to the two groups should be as random as possible, nevertheless, to avoid errors creeping in.

Levels of measurement

When an observation or experiment is completed there will be data. If the data are numerical they can be considered to have different levels of precision. If we categorise people as smokers or non-smokers or if we consider French, German and English people, we cannot put a numerical value on these categories. They are just names. Such data are nominal. The order of finalists in a beauty contest or the rating we give to different types of beer will give us mathematical data. These we can put in rank order, but we cannot say precisely how much more one is preferred than another. We just know their relative position. These data are ordinal. Where we have scores from a test, for example an IQ test or a test of neuroticism. the data are in units. We can assume each unit on the scale is of equal size. These are interval data.

> Nominal – data in categories and a measure of frequency.
> Ordinal – data that can be put in rank order.
> Interval – data measured on a scale of equal units.

Nominal data When data are not numerical as such, and cannot be put into rank order, then they are *nominal*. In other words things are just named or put into categories. Examples would include smokers and non-smokers; males and females; vegetarians, fish eaters and meat eaters. In the picture above, the categories might be 'neat' and 'scruffy'.

Ordinal data When it is possible to put data into ranks, then they are *ordinal*. This is when it is possible to talk about degrees of something. A beauty contest sorts the contestants into order of beauty, as decided by the judges, but although they may be 'first', 'second' and 'third', this does not mean that you can say exactly *how much* more beautiful one is than another. Similarly, we can arrange people according to their height. If we just talk of short, medium and tall, then these are ordinal data. If, however, we actually measure them, in centimetres or inches, then the data are of a more precise nature and are called *interval*.

There is a fourth type of data, ratio, which is where the scale is interval, but where there is an absolute zero. Time is an example, as is length and weight. It is very doubtful that any psychological test produces ratio data.

Interval Data Where data are made up of numbers that come from a scale of equal intervals, then these are *interval* data. In the cartoon, the intervals are hamburgers and a less bizarre example would be inches, or seconds, or grams. It is debatable whether any purely psychological measures can be considered to produce truly interval data. However, scores on personality inventories and IQ tests are treated as interval data, and many psychology experiments do result in measures of time, which are interval. Deciding whether data have reached interval status, if they are in terms of scores from some psychological test, is not always easy. In writing a practical report, your choice in this regard will often need to be justified.

Normal Curve of Distribution

When the distribution of a variable like height is investigated in a population a characteristic type of distribution is found. This is the normal curve of distribution. It has a bell shape because most people are around average height, with only a few who are very short and a few who are very tall. The same kind of distribution would be found for other continuous variables, like IQ scores or scores on a personality inventory.

The curve of this type of distribution has certain very important mathematical properties. When data have been drawn from a population and are continuous (or at an interval level), then certain inferences can be made. This is because the data on populations tend to follow certain fixed boundaries or parameters. Hence, tests that use the predictive properties of the normal curve of distribution are called parametric tests.

Parametric and Non-Parametric Tests

Parametric tests can use the properties of the normal curve of distribution and the related characteristics of the standard deviation. For a test to be parametric it must meet three criteria, relating to (a) the level of measurement, (b) the variance and (c) the type of distribution. Remember that tests are inferring either differences between data or relationships (correlation) between data. To use parametric tests, the data must, in effect, relate to 'populations'. If they do not, or if the two sets of data have very different parameters (ie come from very dissimilar populations), then non-parametric tests must be used.

Parametric tests require		
(1) Data	–	that are at least of interval status
(2) Distribution	–	two sets of scores that conform closely to the normal curve of distribution
(3) Variability	–	both sets of scores having a similar variance (or standard deviation).

Parametric tests	*Non-Parametric tests*
Related t-test	Wilcoxon (also Sign test)
Independent t-test	Mann-Whitney
Pearson's Product Moment	Spearman's rho
	Chi^2

Robustness and Sensitivity

Finally, before considering in detail how to choose a test, their relative merits should be considered. Obviously, the more the smaller variables in data can be monitored or registered by a test, the more sensitive a test will be. On these grounds the Chi^2 test and the Sign test are quite crude. However, it is very difficult to get 'ideal' data that completely meet the requirements of mathematical theory. So, tests that can handle data which are a bit 'rough and ready' are known as robust.

Statisticians debate at great length the relative merits of parametric and non-parametric tests. Generally though, the principle holds that the non-parametric tests are more robust, whilst the parametric tests are more sensitive. The sensitivity of parametric tests means that they are also more powerful.

Choosing statistics for your study

In order to do this you will need to decide or establish answers to the following:

1 Is your study an **experiment** or an **observation**?

While an observation needs to be systematic, with an hypothesis, it will not be structured, with a clear design and manipulation of the independent variable, as in an experiment.

2 If it is an experiment what is the **design**?

Is it **one-group/matched groups** involving **repeated measures** or is it **two groups** involving **independent measures**?
Or
is it a **non-causal** design, investigation **association** or **correlation**?

3 Is the **hypothesis** you are using **one-tailed** or **two-tailed**?

If you are predicting that the independent variable will affect the dependent variable in a particular way (eg specifying 'greater' or 'lesser'), then it is a **one-tailed hypothesis**. Otherwise it is **two-tailed**.

4 What level of **data** has your experiment produced?

Nominal – names or classification into categories eg smokers, non-smokers.
Ordinal – data that can be put in *rank order* eg judgements of attractiveness.
Interval – where the units of measurement are of *equal dimension* eg IQ scores
Ratio – the same as interval data but with an '*absolute zero* ' eg time.

5 Are the data suitable for a **parametric** test?

To be suitable the data must:
– be at least **interval** status
– be **normally** distributed
– have very similar **variance**

6 What **descriptive** statistics are appropriate?

Raw data in a report need to be presented in an organised form:
– bar charts, pie charts, graphs, scattergrams; tables of data;
– measures of central tendency,

the **mean, median** and **mode**;
– measures of dispersion, the
**variance, standard deviation,
range**.

7 What **inferential** statistics
can be used (if any)?

Choice of **parametric** or
non-parametric tests.

8 What **level of significance**
has been chosen?

What probability level is
appropriate for the experiment?

*These criteria can now be applied to the flow chart below to decide which
statistics test is appropriate for the experiment.*

Choosing the Statistical test

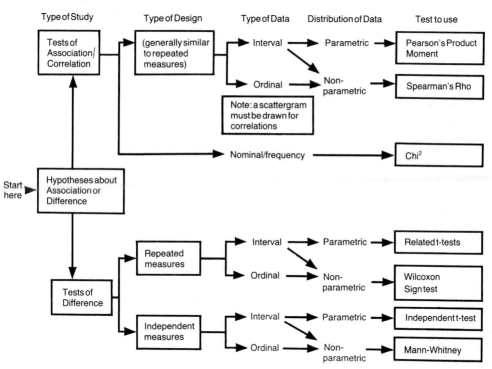

Writing up the psychology practical

Having successfully completed a piece of practical work, it is then necessary to produce a report. This requires both a specific format and a certain style of writing. The approach is different to the style that you may use in essays. Also the order in which you write about things needs to be standardised. This will be dealt with below. With regard to the style, you will need to adopt an impersonal phraseology. Instead of saying 'I did such and such', you need to use phrases like 'the experimenter did . . .'. Avoid saying 'we found that . . .' and say rather 'the experiment showed that . . .' or 'it was observed that . . .'.

What follows is a checklist of points that you need to cover in a report. As the reports form part of the examination assessment, you need to ensure that you cover all the parts of all the sections in your writing or you run the risk of losing marks. Each heading below should form part of your account. However some adjustments need to be made for observational studies.

Abstract

This is a *brief* summary of the *whole* report – 100 to 150 words maximum. It should touch on:

the problem being investigated

type of experimental method/design

subjects – who?
– how many?
– how selected?

IV and DV or variables in correlation/observation

experimental hypothesis (not word for word, but summarised).

main results – literally in a sentence;
– statistical test used, if any
– significant or not at what level

Introduction

This introduces the area you are studying, and your particular experiment. It is mainly a *critical* summary of related studies. It should deal with:

relevant theory

relevant studies, with names/dates/basic findings

studies/theory relating to your *actual* IV/DV (eg if gender is a variable then gender must be dealt with to some extent in the introduction) if yours is a modification of an existing experiment give sufficient detail about this original experiment

make a link from the general introduction to what your experiment will focus upon

briefly introduce the key point/line/emphasis of your experiment

the aims of your experiment must be clarified here

brief details of pilot study could be given here (or in methods section, as appropriate), if one was undertaken

Method

The method section of the report consists of a number of subsections. Try to ensure that you do not repeat yourself in these sections. The procedure in particular should be kept to its own section and not allowed to spill over into the description of the design.

Design

State type of practical ie observation or experiment; correlation or inferential etc.

State design eg repeated measures, independent measures etc.

Very brief explanation as to *why* this design was chosen (no more than a sentence).

Variables (even in an observation and correlation)
  – IV
  – DV
  Be precise; your definition of variables must be in terms of what actually varied (eg the *increase* in . . .; the *score* attained . . .)
  – Very brief reference to scoring/measurement used (eg score on personality test; number of dots made in one minute . . .)

State experimental hypothesis
This should be constructed in terms of the IV and DV where appropriate. It should be one concise sentence.

State Null Hypothesis
This should also relate to the IV and DV but indicate that no *significant relationship* is expected.

Controls used should be outlined here – detail can appear in procedure, if necessary (eg mention that design was *counterbalanced*; mention age/sex controlled for etc).

Subjects

The number of subjects (and the population they represent, where appropriate)

Gender; age; class/educational background (as appropriate)

How selected

Apparatus

List all the materials, equipment used

Diagrams where necessary

If schedules/tests used, either reproduce here or in appendix

Procedure

This section should be a simple, very concise, step by step summary of what the experimenter(s) and subjects had to do. All specific instructions given should be reproduced in full.

Experimental conditions; time of day, noise levels etc

Detail of controls as necessary

State instructions clearly, eg in speech marks

State how any unforseen problems were coped with

Results

This is a *summary* of your data – **not** all the raw data. It should be presented in a clear format, which relates to the hypothesis that you are testing. Usually there should be both a table of results and a graph.

The table to have a proper title and labels

Usually give the totals/means

If there are a lot of raw data, then simplify and summarise as appropriate

Put full raw data in appendix

Any graphs drawn must be graphs! In other words the two axes should show some sort of variable/variation. *Do not plot raw data subject by subject.* . Where it is illustrative, the subjects may be put in rank order for one of the variables and plotted against the other variable.

Graph should have clear title and labels

Graph can be line, histogram or scattergram

Use colour or neat shading where necessary, to show comparisons

Graphs must show *patterns* or *trends* – do not draw just to fill up space

You should provide a short explanation of any graphs or tables

At the end of your summary of results you may comment (one or two sentences at the most) on what the results appear to show. Then go onto the statistical test.

Explain *why* you chose this statistical test in relation to:

Test of association or difference

Type of data

Parametric or non-parametric

Give relevant details, for example:

The statistical value obtained from the test (calculated value)

The critical value needed to meet the level of significance

The level of significance obtained (or not) eg $p = 0.05$

A brief comment on the level of significance obtained 0.05 or 0.025 or 0.01 or higher

Either here, or in the design section, put the level of significance that you are taking as being significant for your hypothesis. This relates to the issue of Type I and Type II errors. Basically, you need to state whether a probablilty of 0.05 is sufficient to reject the Null Hypothesis, or whether 0.01 is needed.

With an observation or a practical that does not involve statistics, the results section should be used to present your findings in as imaginative and illustrative a way as possible. Use diagrams, quotations, pictures, descriptions or whatever is helpful, to summarise what your investigation revealed.

Give a very brief conclusion (one or two sentences).

Discussion

This section is important and should be written with great care. You must ensure that you cover all the following:

A statement of what your results showed (one or two sentences)
This statement will generally mention the statistical test, the calculated and critical values, and the significance level used/obtained. State whether the Null Hypothesis or the Experimental Hypothesis was rejected.

Then discuss any other features of your findings (trends, key results, aspects of graphs etc)

Highlight any particularly notable results

How do your results relate to the general theory/experimental background outlined in your introduction? This *must* be fully discussed. Refer to relevant studies and show how your work extends, supports or contradicts

Critically review the methodological weaknesses of your experiment (apparatus, procedure, controls, sample etc)

In relation to this, thoroughly consider the question of reliability and validity of your measures of your variables

Suggest reasonable modifications/extensions (not just 'a bigger sample would have produced a significant result')

Comment on the statistical procedures used – particularly the issue of the *power* of the test and the *sensitivity* of the test. Round off with a very brief conclusion, restating the hypothesis that was supported – and *not* using the word 'proof' or its derivatives

Designing and writing up a practical – three examples

In this section we will consider three practical reports. In the first we will look in detail at how the practical can be developed from an initial idea to its final written form. Then two further practical reports will be presented, with a commentary on each.

A practical on feedback

As suggested earlier in the book (pages 43–45) there are various stages to planning a practical. The first is to choose a suitable problem to study. In the example presented here, the choice is to consider the concept of *reinforcement*, which is part of Learning Theory. More specifically, we choose to look at *feedback* as an aspect of reinforcement. Having settled on an idea, the next step is to decide on a working hypothesis, which will guide the research. This can be simply stated as 'feedback will aid the learning process of a simple task'. This working hypothesis will allow you to search the relevant text books to see if there is sufficient background material to provide a theoretical basis for an experiment in this area. Most general texts have considerable space devoted to the topic of reinforcement in general and some material on feedback as such. In addition any specialist books on learning theory will have more detailed information.

Having scanned the texts, it becomes possible to choose the actual way in which the concept of feedback can be 'operationalised' into something that can be actually tested. There are many ways in which this could be done. One of the simplest is to set up a situation in which there is feedback against one in which there is not. The task could be anything that allowed reasonably accurate measurement. For example, inviting subjects to try to control the temperature of their fingertips. This could be measured with a sensitive thermometer. Even simpler, is a task that involves drawing a line of a given length. The feedback would be in terms of by how far the line was drawn inaccurately.

Having chosen the task, a suitable design needs to be selected. The independent variable in this experiment will be whether feedback is given or not. The dependent variable will be the accuracy with which the line is drawn. It would be possible, with counterbalancing, to use a repeated measures design. However, an independent measures design, using two groups will be used. This is chosen because a repetitive activity like drawing a line could prove boring if subjects had to do it too many times under the two different conditions.

A suitable size of sample also needs to be selected. Ten subjects under each condition should be sufficient to see if there is an effect.

The apparatus required will be sufficient sheets of blank paper, cut into squares of about three inches. A pencil, a ruler and a sheet to record results, will be necessary, along with a sheet of standardised instructions. It will be helpful to carry out a brief pilot study to see if the method chosen actually works.

The data are going to be in terms of length. That is, the degree to which the lines drawn are inaccurate. The data therefore will be interval. If they prove to be parametric, then it will be possible to do an independent t-test (see page 67). If not, then a Mann-Whitney will be chosen. The level of significance selected for this experiment, will be $p \leqslant 0.05$ for a one-tailed test.

The effect of feedback on the accuracy of performing a manual skill

The title should be informative about the nature of the study without being overlong.

Abstract

This study tests the concept of feedback, in terms of information given to subjects about a manual task they are to perform. 20 subjects were chosen through an opportunity sample. They were all college students. Using an independent measures design the experimental group were given feedback over their accuracy of drawing a line, the control group were not. A Mann-Whitney test showed that the degree of error was significantly different in the two groups, at a significance level of $p \leqslant 0.05$, for a one-tailed test.

The abstract should be short and entirely to the point. The reader needs to know the purpose of the experiment, the design, and the basic results.

Introduction

When carrying out almost any activity animals and humans receive feedback. In this sense 'feedback' means information concerning the action undertaken. An airline pilot monitoring the dials of his controls and the schoolgirl receiving a mark for her French exam, are both obtaining feedback. This information allows them to adjust their behaviour. As such the information can support what they are doing (positive reinforcement) or indicate a change is necessary (negative reinforcement).

Even if the term that is central to your study is quite well known, it is helpful to provide a brief definition, relevant to your study.

The concept of feedback is a central part of cybernetic theory, which considers how systems (animate and inanimate) can be self-controlling. In this theory a positive feedback will tend to continue or enhance an action or behaviour, a negative feedback will decrease or stop or reverse the original response. The homeostatic mechanisms of the

Having defined terms in the first paragraph, this second paragraph begins to put the terms in context.

body utilise feedback systems to keep aspects of the body's functioning, like temperature, at a constant level.

In learning a skill, the necessity of feedback becomes apparent. It is much easier·to accurately draw with eyes open than with eyes closed, because of the visual feedback. If the skill is control over autonomic responses, then such feedback becomes essential. Studies of *biofeedback* have shown that autonomic responses can be controlled voluntarily. Miller and Dicara (1967) demonstrated this with rats. Their work with paralysed rats has been criticised and has proved difficult to replicate (Walker, 1984). However, this work stimulated much further research into biofeedback. There has been some success with reducing high blood pressure (Blanchard and Young, 1974).

Specific examples are important, but need not be dealt with at great length.

Give some names and dates to back up the points that you are making about studies. However, it is more important that you develop the concepts relevant to *your* study, than to provide a long list of studies.

The concept of feedback is important also in the field of training. Here it is called 'knowledge of results'. It has been classified by Holding (1965) as artificial or intrinsic, verbal or non-verbal, terminal or concurrent. Feedback which occurs during the training period can produce dramatic increases in accuracy (Annett, 1969). The more detailed the feedback that is given, the more accurate the response tends to be.

During training, feedback provides a monitoring function (Bartlett, 1947) and is the essence of a skill, as compared to a habit. When learning a skill, the type of feedback needed tends to be different from the phase of improving or mastering a skill. The early stages require a verbal feedback which enables verbal-motor control (Adams, 1971). Later, motor control takes over. The classic example, is learning to drive. Initially, verbal directions from the instructor are vital. After the basics have been mastered, the feedback comes intrinsically from the bodily-muscular sensations involved in the various aspects of driving, and visual feedback, in terms of where the car is headed!

This work is of direct relevance to the actual study covered in this report. Your introduction should gradually focus in precisely on your aim and purpose.

Aim

The aim of this experiment, is to look at the value of verbal feedback in a simple training situation. The task chosen, is drawing freehand, as accurately as possible, a 10 cm line. The conditions are also simple, involving the presence or absence of verbal feedback. The expectation is that verbal feedback will produce greater accuracy, and a diminishment of error.

A brief statement of your aim is essential. This is different from the hypothesis, and rather provides the general background for the specific hypothesis.

Method

Design

The experiment used two groups. The design was independent measures, with the experimental group receiving feedback and the control group receiving no feedback.

The independent variable (IV) is whether the group received feedback or not.

The dependent variable (DV) is the degree of error, measured in millimetres, for drawing an 10 cm line.

The experimental hypothesis is that receiving feedback in terms of degree of error, will significantly reduce the error as measured in millimetres, when drawing a line of a given length.

The null hypothesis is that feedback will have no significant effect on the degree of error, as measured in millimetres, when drawing a line of a given length.

The controls for the experiment were:
1 using standardised instructions
2 using identical apparatus for each subject
3 using subjects of a similar age and educational background
4 random allocation of subjects to the two groups
5 testing subjects in a similar environment

Do state how many groups are involved in a design. Then give the type of design.

By clarifying the IV and then the DV, it makes the hypothesis, which is essentially the relationship between the two, easier to formulate.

Remember to state that in the null hypothesis there will be no *significant* difference, not that there will be no difference.

Subjects

Twenty subjects were used. They were all college students. There were 12 females and 8 males. The subjects were chosen as an opportunity sample. They were randomly allocated to the two groups by alternating the allocation of subjects to each group as they were chosen. There were two experimenters.

It is helpful to state the number of experimenters involved in an experiment.

Apparatus

1 200 pieces of paper about three inch square
2 one pencil and one pencil sharpener
3 one ruler
4 standardised verbal instructions
5 a record sheet

Procedure

1 A subject was chosen and asked to participate in the psychology experiment. If they agreed they came to a small room and sat at a table. They were allocated to the experimental group or the control as appropriate.

Where allocation to groups is more elaborate, then the procedure should be explained at this stage.

2 The subject was read the following instructions:
'I would like you to draw a line ten centimetres long on the pieces of paper that I will give you. Please start your line at the cross that I draw on the paper. I will/will not give you feedback on how close your line is to ten centimetres.'

If instructions are long they can be put in the appendix.

3 The subject drew the line.
4 The paper was removed, the line measured and its length recorded on the record sheet.
5 Feedback was given to the experimental group in terms of the number of millimetres their line was short or long. No feedback was given to the control group.
6 The procedure was repeated ten times with each subject.
7 The purpose of the experiment was explained to the subject and then they were thanked for their participation.

Always debrief your subjects. This is more than just courtesy, it is the only ethical way of proceeding.

Results

Table showing mean error of subjects, measured in millimetres.

Make sure all your tables have a suitable heading.

Feedback group		Non-feedback group	
S1	9.0	S11	18.6
S2	7.3	S12	12.9
S3	5.4	S13	6.4
S4	6.7	S14	10.7
S5	10.9	S15	14.5
S6	2.7	S16	26.3
S7	10.1	S17	29.9
S8	3.7	S18	5.5
S9	8.2	S19	23.1
S10	9.4	S20	21.0
Total:	73.4	168.9	
Mean:	7.34 mm	16.89 mm	

In this table the degree of error made by each subject is shown, calculated by adding the mean of all their errors together, but ignoring whether the error was of positive or negative value. It is clear that the non-feedback group had a considerably greater margin of error. (For raw data see appendix.)

Give sufficient explanation of a table to make its meaning clear. A brief one sentence comment may be appropriate.

A graph showing the mean error of each of the subjects, for each trial, taking account of the sign.

Be sure that your graphs have an adequate heading, and that each axis is labelled.

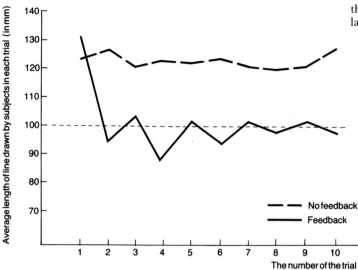

The points on this graph are calculated by adding the error for each subject for each trial, taking account of the sign (direction of error) and calculating the mean for each group. (See appendix for calculations.)

Again, a very brief comment may be of value, to indicate what the graph is illustrating.

The graph shows the effect of giving feedback. There is a clear tendency for the results of the experimental group to ossilate around the 100 mm line. The control group consistently overestimates the length of the line.

Statistical test and level of significance

The level of significance chosen is $p \leq 0.05$. This is by convention. The data are of at least interval status. However, they are not normally distributed and so a Mann-Whitney test was carried out. This test is appropriate or an independent measures design on data of at least ordinal status.

If you choose another level of significance, say 0.01, you need to explain why (possibly in terms of avoiding a Type I error).

The value of U was found to be = 15. This is significant for a one-tailed test at $p \leq 0.005$. The null hypothesis is therefore rejected and the experimental hypothesis supported.

Be sure to specify one or two tailed, for the test.

Discussion

The results of the Mann-Whitney test indicated that feedback is important in producing accuracy in a manual task. The experimental hypothesis was supported, and the probability

It is not obligatory, but it is helpful, to start by considering the actual results achieved.

level achieved of 0.005, suggested strong support for the hypothesis. The other aspect of the study, that the effect of feedback would be cumulative, with a diminishment in error, was not framed specifically as an hypothesis. There is support for this provided by the graph. This indicates that the feedback group, which had an error in the first trial greater than the control group, achieved a greater accuracy by the second trial, which they were able to maintain. The results of the feedback group show that they tended to ossilate around the 10 cm line. The non-feedback group remained generally 2 cm away from the line. The raw data (given in the appendix) demonstrate the considerably greater erratic nature of the control group's results.

The findings indicated by tables or graphs, should be briefly commented upon.

Although the results were significant, the test was not the most sensitive that could be used. The Mann-Whitney test is not as precise as the t-test. A higher level of significance might have been achieved with that test, had the results been fully parametric. A further analysis of the results to demonstrate the degree to which the experimental group learned over successive trials could also have been undertaken. The graph indicates that this is so, but a comparison of the degree of error in trials 2 to 5 with those in 6 to 10, would demonstrate if this was significant. A Wilcoxon test could have been used on the data from the experimental group alone.

Descriptive and inferential statistics both have room for error. The discussion should consider the likelihood of this error. Sometimes it can be that a test has not produced a significant result, but that it is clear that a more sensitive measure would be likely to do so. For example a sign test may not be significant, where a Wilcoxon test is significant.

In general, the results of this experiment give support to the idea that feedback is necessary in training. Without knowledge of results (Holding), there is little possibility of the control group becoming more accurate. The only way they could become better would be if they do have an accurate notion of the length of a ten centimetre line, but need *practice* to learn to draw it accurately using freehand. This did not prove to be the case.

Make specific links back to studies or theories mentioned in the introduction.

The need for verbal-motor control, as suggested by Adams, during the early stages of learning a skill, is supported. Annett's suggestion that giving feedback concurrently with performance also appears to be supported, although it could be argued that the feedback was given at the end of each individual 'performance'.

You should be as rigorous as you can be in critically assessing what your results do, and do not, show.

The value of feedback does appear to be sustained in this study. However, some questions are raised. There is a confounding variable. Not only did the experimental group receive feedback, they also necessarily and at the same time received a verbal commentary on their work. The control group had only silence. This in itself could be considered a positive reinforcement, and consequently, the experimental group may have tried harder. The study could therefore have been measuring the effect of encouragement rather than the pure effect of information.

If you become aware of a weakness in your study then this is the place to explore it. You will not lose marks for spotting a flaw in an otherwise effective design.

This criticism could be met by a different way of conducting the experiment. Instead of the control group receiving no feedback, they could be told that their line was too big, or too small. This would be contrasted with the experimental group, who would be informed by how much their line was too big or too small. Both would be receiving feedback (and possibly positive reinforcement) but the experimental group would have more accurate feedback, enabling the hypothesis to be tested.

You need to comment on two aspects of your work. The first is the way in which your study could be modified to ensure that it measures what it is setting out to measure more effectively.

Another criticism of the experiment, is the problem of boredom. Subjects did appear to find the task a little tedious and perhaps did not concentrate. Although this was controlled for by keeping the task the same for both groups, a more interesting task could have been chosen.

A modification that could follow from this, would be to choose a task that is inherently more interesting. A computer game could be used, and played under two conditions, with sound on or with sound off. This would be appropriate, if the game led to a score that could be compared, and if the sound changed in a way that provided feedback to enable the game to be played more skilfully. Another possibility would be to take a manual and conceptual skill like solving a simple puzzle. The two conditions could involve different types of feedback which could be compared.

The second aspect is how could your work be extended. Here you will be looking not so much at improvements in technique as ways in which the concepts could be elaborated or explored in more depth. The suggestions made should be feasible and appropriate for this level of work.

References

Legge D and Barber P *Information and Skill*, Methuen 1976
  Cybernetics (pp 66–70) Holding; Annett; Adams (pp 122–116)

Gross R *Psychology*, Edward Arnold, 1987
  Biofeedback (pp 414–415)

Atkinson R, Atkinson R and Hilgard E *Introduction to Psychology* Harcourt Brace Jovanovitch 1883
  Biofeedback (pp 207–208)

Gleitman *Psychology*, Norton, 1981
  Negative and positive feedback (pp 57–58)

Appendix

No appendix will be given here for reasons of space, but all the raw data and the workings of the Mann-Whitney test would be in the appendix.

An experiment to discover if a female is more inhibited by a male stranger than a female stranger in a secluded situation requiring cooperation

Abstract

The alternate hypothesis was, 'Women are less likely to air opinions or theories and are generally more inhibited in the company of a male stranger than in that of a female stranger'. The null hypothesis denied the possibility of such a difference. The hypotheses were one-tailed as they stated a difference (in the null) between the two conditions and also stated the direction of the difference. The experiment was pure observation, so no factual raw data were produced therefore no test can be applied to it.(1)

The subjects were paired off. All pairs were strangers to one another. Half the pairs were male/female pairs, the other half were female/female pairs. They all attempted the Wason's Rule Problem(2) and the behaviour of the female within the pair was observed whilst they did so.

The data recorded on the observation sheet appeared to suggest that the female is more inhibited generally by a male stranger than a female stranger.

(1) This is an unusual study, in so far as the experimenter chose an experimental situation as a cover for his observation.

(2) Wason's Rule Problem is a problem in logic, which, though simple, often proves difficult for adults to solve logically.

Introduction

This experiment centres around the sex roles in society and their effect on the female. Many of the psychologists and sociologists studying woman call for the need for a distinction between 'sex' and 'gender'. Sex is the maleness or femaleness in biological terms. However, gender refers to the interaction between biological endowment and the social influence on the individual. The definition of the 'sex role' by Spence, Helmreich and Deaux (1983) incorporates both of these. They said sex roles are behaviour patterns that characterise people or that are expected of them on the basis of their biological sex. They said there is still pressure on men and women to behave differently according to their sex.(3)

Sex-role concepts and stereotypes are developed by children observing and imitating more senior models. Thus, the children develop ideas about the types of behaviour that are 'expected' of men and women. In other words, they learn the role associated with their gender. Within Bem and Bem's Non-Conscious Ideology they included the prejudice against the woman by society. But in relation to the whole of this ideology, they said the specific beliefs were inbuilt in society to the extent that people are brought up surrounded by them and cannot imagine any other way.

There is some minor disagreement as to the start of sex-role concepts and stereotypes by children. Kuhn, Nash and

(3) As the observation is about behaviour relating to gender, the writer correctly makes this his starting point in his introduction.

Brucken (1978) said the signs of such developments began at around three years old. Harley disagreed, saying the age was more like five years. Whatever the age at which they begin, such sex-role concepts and stereotypes are made up of the same beliefs and assumptions. Aronson said the male is traditionally the breadwinner; aggressive, clever and creative. Females are highly anxious and of low self-esteem. Best showed that by the fifth grade, children saw women as weak, softhearted and sentimental and men as strong, robust, aggressive, assertive, cruel and dominant.

The generally 'negative' and 'inferior' characteristics associated with the female sex were seen to be taken 'on board' in a study by Feldman and Kiesler. They showed that male undergraduates attributed a female physicians success to luck and an easier path, believing her to be less competent than a male physician. Female undergraduates thought the opposite. Interestingly, all the subjects thought the female to be more motivated, presumably because she had to break free of her expected lifestyle.

Aronson said, within society, women, just like other minority groups, are rewarded for actions that make them appear inferior, passive, dependent and neurotic. He said this leads to a self-fulfilling prophecy (ie treatment of women in society affects and determines the way they look at themselves). He said if women try to see themselves in a capacity outside their expected behaviour they will experience discomfort because their behaviour differs from their self concept, developed since childhood. Deaux and Emswiller showed that subjects attributed male student success to ability and female student success to luck. Nicholls went further to theorise that this extends to a woman's self-attributions (as stated by Aronson). He showed that in the fourth grade, boys attributed their good results to their ability and bad results to their bad luck, whereas girls attributed good results less to ability and bad results to a lack of ability.**(4)**

(4) While this material on sex-role stereotyping is relevant, it is questionable whether this much detail is necessary here. The writer is drifting away from the main issue in the observation, which is the question of whether females are more inhibited by male or female strangers.

There is a trend for the sex stereotypes of women to be decreasing. Lipman-Blumen said the more the decrease continues, the more women there will be entering higher education.

The attempt of this experiment is to show if the weaker and dominated role of the woman is a reality when in the company of male strangers. (Obviously women should be less inhibited by personally-known males.)**(5)**

(5) This makes an important connection back to the problem that is being addressed in this study.

Operationalising this experiment involves producing a condition where a male and a female are placed in a secluded setting in a situation requiring cooperation and communication. The role the woman takes should be analysed. This is done using a female stranger also, to produce a comparison.**(6)**

(6) Here the actual experiment itself is introduced. There is no need to go into the whole procedure, but it is helpful to highlight the approach that is to be taken in the study.

This is quite simple to do. A male and female, without having met before, are placed together in a private room and are asked to solve Wason's Rule Problem. This should be adequate as a situation. The analysis of the woman's role should be based on Bales' Interaction Process Analysis. This is a system of category scoring for coding verbal interactions in small group settings, the categories are: positive reactions, questions, attempted answers and negative reactions, each split into three.

Emotional area positive reaction	1 Shows solidarity
	2 Shows tension release
	3 Agrees – passively
Task area attempted answers	4 Gives suggestion
	5 Gives opinion
	6 Gives orientation
Task area questions	7 Asks for orientation
	8 Asks for opinion
	9 Asks for suggestion
Emotional area negative reaction	10 Disagrees
	11 Shows tension
	12 Shows antagonism

Such a method should show the effect of the male on the female's behaviour, relative to another female.**(7)**

Method

Design

The null hypothesis for this experiment is:

'Women are not less likely to air opinions and theories and generally will not be more inhibited in the company of a male stranger than that of a female stranger'.

The alternate hypothesis for the experiment is:

'Women are less likely to air opinions and theories and generally will be more inhibited in the company of a male stranger than that of a female stranger'.**(8)**

The Alternate Hypothesis is 'one-tailed' because it predicts a difference between the two conditions and predicts the direction of the difference.

(7) It is particularly appropriate to mention a specific technique that is going to be used in the study, in the context of operationalisation. In other words how a theoretical idea is going to be made measurable. The actual procedural details can be dealt with later.

(8) It is not always possible in an observation, to come up with a specific hypothesis in terms of measurable variables. Here, although the technique being used is observation, nevertheless two distinct conditions are being observed.

The Independent Variable for this experiment consists of two conditions, the company of a male stranger and the company of a female stranger.

The Dependent Variable for this experiment consists of the behaviour of a female in both conditions.

The design of the experiment is independent groups, as one subject cannot take part in both conditions of the IV. However, the data are pure observation and the factual data produced directly by the subjects. Therefore it is not really possible to apply any statistical test.

The controls of the experiment were quite numerous. All pairs were strangers whether they were male/female or female/female pairs. This was in order to avoid the possibility of a subject being less inhibited because they knew the other person. All the pairs performed in the same environment (room), with no prompting by the experimenter or external stimuli. The problem to solve was identical for all pairs, as were the instructions on how to achieve a solution. Age was controlled for (all the subjects were of the same age bracket) in case it had an effect on the women's behaviour. The same applies to race (all subjects were white). No order or practice effects are possible as the subjects only perform in one of the conditions, and only once.

Apparatus – the following equipment is required:
Sheet explaining Wason's Rule Problem
Observation sheet
Stop-Watch
Three chairs and one desk

Subjects
The subjects are all white and aged between 17 and 20 years old. They were all from south east Essex. Half the subjects were taken from the South East Essex Sixth Form College where they are studying for 'A' levels, the other half from various occupations. There were 15 female subjects and 5 male subjects. All the subjects were working class or middle class.

Procedure(9)

1 The pair is shown into the experimental room.
2 They are told to be seated and given the sheet showing the Wason's Rule Problem – this is self explanatory.
3 The pair is told they have a maximum of five minutes to solve the problem.
4 As the subjects attempt to solve the problem, the behaviour of the female should be observed and the appropriate behaviours ticked on the observation sheet.

(9) It is quite acceptable for the procedure to be written as a series of points. What is important is, whether another person could easily perform the experiment with these as guidelines.

(If the pair is all-female, one female should have been randomly chosen as the female to be observed).

5 If the subjects attempt an answer that is correct, tell them so and stop the observation. If it is not, tell them it is wrong and to continue.

6 When the pair has completed the problem, or the five minutes are up, the observation sheet should show the behaviour of the female subject.

7 Repeat for all ten pairs.

8 The completed data may be recorded and drawn graphically.

(10) The table shows event sampling for the females in the pairs. It enables a comparison to be made of the various factors that were observed.

Results(10)

Female/Male pairs

	Pair No.					Total
	1	2	3	4	5	
positive reaction – Give opinions	5	5	1	3	4	18
Attempted answer	2	1	0	3	3	9
Solidarity – help	1	0	0	1	3	5
Show Tension – withdraw	3	3	1	1	4	12
Passive/agree/ comply	4	1	0	2	5	12
Time elapsed (min/sec)	5/00	4/21	2/15	5/00	5/00	21/36

Female/Female pairs

	Pair No.					Total
	1	2	3	4	5	
positive reaction – Give opinions	4	3	9	4	2	22
Attempted answer	2	3	4	1	1	11
Solidarity – help	4	2	5	2	0	13
Show Tension – withdraw	1	0	1	0	1	3
Passive/agree/ comply	2	1	0	2	6	11
Time elapsed (min/sec)	3/52	4/26	5/00	5/00	5/00	23/18

The tables above show the results received from arranging either male/female or female/female pairs (in which the subjects have never met) and asking them to solve the Wason's Rule Problem. The role of the female in both types of pairs can be observed and actions categorised and then tallied.

The overall tendencies can be drawn graphically:**(11)**

(11) Even when a table is quite simple, a graphical representation is valuable. Here it highlights the main situations where there were differences between the two conditions.

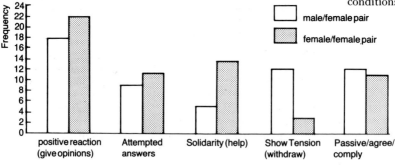

However as the total time shows, the two conditions were not observed for equal time periods for all 5 pairs. This was because observation stopped if the pair discovered the solution. Thus, this is not a true comparison.

One way to discover a true comparison would be to take the overall frequencies of behaviour from each condition and to divide by the amount of seconds for which each condition was observed.

This was: Male/female pairs   – 1296 seconds
Female/female pairs – 1398 seconds

This produces the following graph:**(12)**

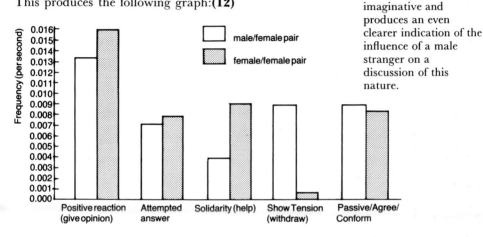

(12) This further reworking of the data is imaginative and produces an even clearer indication of the influence of a male stranger on a discussion of this nature.

The data are pure observation by the experimenter so no particular statistical test can be applied to them.

Discussion

No one, single result can be concluded from the observation regarding the difference in the female's behaviour with a male stranger to that with a female stranger. Some of the results appear to make the Alternate Hypothesis acceptable.**(13)** This is because the context in which the basis of the hypothesis is put is crucial. Women were significantly inhibited by the males relative to the females in the context of helping their partner and withdrawing after disagreement or criticism from the partner. The help given to male partners was minimal and withdrawal after male criticism was greater. However, in the context of airing opinions and theories (attempted answers), the presence of a male stranger did not significantly inhibit the female subject, relative to a female stranger. In both cases, they still put over fewer opinions and theories with the male stranger, but only just. Also the tendency to comply with male strangers' ideas was not greater than with female strangers.**(14)**

(13) The discussion usefully considers the results as a whole in relation to the hypothesis and the overall aims of the observation.

(14) In this first paragraph, it is not a question of repeating the results, but rather reflecting on their *significance*. This is accomplished quite effectively here.

The result was not totally as expected, although in truth, not a great surprise. It showed that women have lost the tendency to be totally dominated by males as in past ages. **(15)** They now air opinions and theories as much with males as fellow females. They are not inhibited in this sense. Also they do not passively comply with males to a significantly greater extent than females as women of previous generations were brought up to do. However, a kind of aura still surrounds the male, it could be said. Women were less frequent in their help for males, they appeared inhibited to do so. Old, traditional values may have said this was because the woman felt unable to help the dominant man. Also, the tendency to back down after arguments with or criticism from males more than after that from females still can be seen. Old values would say this is because the woman feels intimidated more by them and takes more notice.

(15) Assumptions are being made here about 'how females were in the past' that are not supported by evidence or reference to research.

The basic design of the experiment seemed adequate.**(16)** The Bales 'Interaction Process Analysis' seemed to pick up the relevant behaviour quite well, despite the fact the original had been slightly altered. Also, Wason's Rule Problem performed well in producing a response from the subjects. It created sufficient interaction that could be categorised when observed. Such observation may have an experimental effect on the study because the subjects are aware of the observation. However, Wason's problem diverted their attentions totally killing off any possible effect.**(17)**

(16) Here the discussion begins a critical consideration of the techniques and design of the observation.

The subjects were taken half-and-half from SEEVIC College and full-time occupations in the area. This ensured the pairs were strangers, which stopped a confounding effect of familiarity of subjects altering the women's behaviour. However, the experimenter did purposely make up the pairs to ensure they were strangers. Such deliberate pairing may produce an experimenter effect. However this is only possibly via other variables like intelligence and personality. The intelligence of the subjects was not strictly controlled for, although all the subjects were perfectly capable of understanding the problem and attempting a solution, which was considered adequate. Personalities were also left uncontrolled. These may have considerable effects on the behaviour of the women. However, the results were aggregate results from five pairings in each condition. This was thought to sufficiently 'iron-out' personality differences to give an average. Possibly more pairings in each condition may be called for to do this really effectively. Other possible confounding variables, such as class, age and race were all controlled for totally as were any situational variables. Five minutes appeared an adequate length of time for observation. It produced just enough data to show the relevant trends. The subjects were close to finishing the problem and thus stopped the observation after five minutes, by-and-large, anyway.**(18)**

(17) This assumption that there was no 'observer effect', is difficult to justify. It is something that the researcher can never be sure about. The writer should bear in mind that, as a male, he may also have influenced the whole process of the observation.

(18) This section usefully reviews the various controls that were applied and assesses their worth quite effectively.

A criticism may be of the behaviour recordings. These were done by the experimenter, whereas Bales recommends skilled observers. Also, an experimenter bias is possible. However, the basic categories for behaviour were drawn up by the experimenter and adhered to totally.

The experiment has interesting implications. It suggests Aronson was partly right when he said women had low self-esteem.(19) It was low enough to help males less and withdraw more but was high enough to put over many opinions/theories and resist passively complying with males. Also his proposal of a self-fulfillment for women as dominated and inferior, again, is partly supported. They possibly believed within themselves that they should not attempt to help or guide the males and that they should withdraw and be quiet when criticised or disagreed with by a male. However, women did put over numerous opinions, did *not* comply without hesitation or discomfort, contrary to Aronson. Best's experimental findings of the male, thought to be dominant, strong and assertive, and the woman as weak, were also only partly supported. The dominance showed in the withdrawal frequency and reluctance to help, but was totally lacking in the opinions, theories and compliance context. Males did not dominate females at all or intimidate them on any of these accounts.

(19) Now some consideration is given to the relationship between the findings of this observation and general theory.

The implication may be that the rapid increase in women's movements and the fight for sexual equality has given women the presence and confidence to voice their opinions and theories against males and the courage to refrain from conforming to males and accepting their beliefs passively. However, it has not yet reduced the power of the male criticism over women or increased women's confidence and self-esteem to help or guide the male.

Further works on this topic are potentially numerous. Other age groups may be used to show the effects of age on the attitudes and behaviour of women. Also, a personality test may be used to filter out certain types of personality for analysis, rather than women in general (what is thought to produce an 'average personality'). Also, subjects who are not strangers may be used to show the effects of familiarity or friendship on the woman's role or behaviour.

Conclusion

No firm conclusion can be made from the observation but certain tendencies do show through.

1 Male strangers may significantly inhibit females relative to female strangers in certain contexts, but not *all* contexts.

2 The tendency for the traditional female sex-role stereotype to be adhered to is falling and the male dominance is no longer so comprehensive.

References

Raven and Rubin   *Social Psychology* pp 510–520
                     Wiley and Sons Press (1983)

Bee and Mitchell   *The Developing Person*
                    pp 218–219
                    Harper and Row Press (1984)

Aronson E   *The Social Animal*
                    Freeman Press**(20)**

(20) It would be helpful if the references could be a bit fuller, giving more detail on which particular theoretical parts came from which books.

Space does not allow the reproduction of the various appendices that went with this report. They included details of Wason's Rule Problem, more detailed results, reproducing the observation sheets used, and a sketch of the way the subjects and observer were seated.

This observation, or observational experiment, has a number of strong features. The aims and purpose are clear, and appropriate for this level of work. The design and procedure are well thought out and the question of male/female behaviour is effectively operationalised using Bales' categories. The introduction covers both theory and the question of observational technique. The theoretical aspect could have been picked up more fully in the discussion. The results section is well illustrated, and the various charts do demonstrate the patterns that emerged during the observation.

An experiment looking into any bias in the length of prison sentences given to attackers, due to racial prejudice.(1)

(1) Title is clear and indicates area of research.

Abstract

An experiment looking into racial prejudice in prison sentencing.

In the text, subjects were given a description of an attack on a female. In half of the descriptions, the attack was carried out by a black male and in the other half it was carried out by a white male. Subjects had to mark on a scale how long a prison sentence they believed the attacker should receive.

The null hypothesis was that there would be no significant difference in the length of sentences given to black or white male attackers.

Twenty males and twenty females were tested and the experimental design was matched pairs. A Wilcoxon test was applied, resulting in a significant result of 0.025, implying there is racial prejudice involved in prison sentencing.**(2)**

Introduction

Prejudice has become an 'accepted' part of our society and has been described as;

'a hostile or negative attitude towards a distinguishable group based on generalisations derived from faulty or incomplete information.'

(E Aronson)

Most prejudice involves stereotyping, in which people are put into categories, just because they have one characteristic trait of that category and it is then assumed that they also have other traits of people belonging to that category. People can be stereotyped in a positive way, for example, it is often assumed that physically attractive people are also kind and friendly, but, where prejudice is involved, it is normally negative stereotyping that takes place.**(3)**

Racial prejudice is one particular type that seems to be very strong in our society, with many racial attacks being made and the unemployment figure amongst blacks greater than that amongst whites. It seems that prejudice is felt among blacks from a very young age. This was shown by an experiment carried out by Clark and Clark (1947). In this experiment, young black children were given a mixture of black and white dolls. The black dolls were rejected, as it was felt that the white dolls were prettier and superior. When the children were asked which of the dolls was like them, they became confused and frightened. This realisation of prejudice and being unequal from a very young age, could be due to a 'non-conscious ideology', an idea which was put forward by Bem and Bem in 1970. This suggests that people are born into a society full of prejudice and bias and they therefore become prejudiced by living in the society, without really realising it.**(4)**

With this knowledge of prejudice, it would seem that people have no choice but to grow up to be prejudiced in some way, although these feelings may be hidden. Even if people are not prejudiced themselves, it would seem that they are worried about other people being so. This is shown in jobs in which there is a lot of dealing with customers and any black workers have to carry out their work out of sight. For example, a black woman described her job where she made cakes in a cake shop, but was not allowed to serve them as it may put any customers off buying them.

There seems to be a general low opinion felt towards blacks, with people going as far as attacking them just because of the colour of their skin. It would seem logical then,

(2) A brief explanation of the procedure is usefully linked to the null hypothesis. The result is given but should more correctly be expressed p ≤ 0.025

(3) Prejudice, the central concept, is defined effectively, and linked to another key concept, namely stereotyping.

(4) This is one theory of prejudice, suggesting it is learned. Others could be briefly mentioned.

that people would also feel blacks more capable of committing crimes than their white counterparts. This could be due to people feeling they would commit crimes because of the low opinion they have of them or because people feel that due to their position in society, blacks are more likely to commit crimes such as stealing, almost out of necessity. Perhaps then, it would also be felt necessary to give blacks a greater punishment for commiting a crime and this is what the experiment is looking into. Will people actually sentence blacks longer than whites, when exactly the same crime is being committed?**(5)**

(5) While this section does introduce the experiment in a relevant way, it lacks sufficient references to theories and studies.

Design

This experiment is designed to find out whether there is any difference in the length of sentences given to black or white male attackers. It is a matched pairs design.**(6)**

(6) This brief statement of the design is appropriate.

Controls**(7)**

Subjects

All subjects are matched according to age, sex and level of studies. Half are given the description of the attack including the black male and half the description involving the white male.

(7) It is necessary to state the controls used in an experiment, and briefly, why they are used.

Situation

All subjects are tested separately.

Experimenter

There are two experimenters, each using the same amount of male and female subjects and using the same amount of descriptions of the black and the white attacker.

Independent variable

Whether the attacker in the description given was black or white.

Dependent variable

The length of the sentence given.

(8) We would expect a difference in the scores of the two groups, but whether the difference is significant or not, is crucial.

Null hypothesis

'There is no significant**(8)** difference between the length of sentence given to black or white male attackers.'

Alternate hypothesis

'The length of sentence given to black male attackers is significantly longer than that given to white male attackers.'

(This is one-tailed, as it is biased towards black attackers being given a longer sentence than white ones).**(9)**

(9) It is important to state if an hypothesis is one or two-tailed.

Method

Apparatus

– two copies of the story telling the attack, one with a black male attacker, the other with a white male attacker. (See appendix 1.)
– answers sheets (See appendix 2.)
– pen.**(10)**

(10) How much of the apparatus is reproduced here and how much is put in the appendix, is a matter of judgement. Examples or extracts of materials used are appropriate here, if brief.

Subjects

20 males, 20 females
All aged 17 or 18
All studying 'A' levels at South East Essex Sixth
Form College.

They were chosen according to the people available fitting the above description, at the time the experiment was carried out.**(11)**

(11) It is accepted that it is not usually possible to undertake a truly random sample; however, allocation into groups should be controlled eg through randomisation or matching.

Procedure

1 Subjects were tested alone.
2 Each subject was shown a copy of one of the two stories telling the attack (See appendix 1), depending on the group they were assigned to.
3 After reading the story, subjects were asked to mark on a scale how long a sentence they believe the attacker deserved (0–5 years).
4 The same procedure is repeated for all subjects.
5 Tests are applied and conclusion is made.**(12)**

(12) The criterion for a good procedure is whether another can follow it and apply it. The exact instructions to subjects should be included here or in the appendix.

Results

A table to show the length of sentences given to the attacker (in months)**(13)**

	Black		White
S1	36	S2	60
S3	42	S4	60
S5	60	S6	60
S7	60	S8	24
S9	60	S10	24
S11	60	S12	60
S13	60	S14	9
S15	60	S16	24
S17	48	S18	60
S19	60	S20	48
S21	60	S22	48
S23	48	S24	51
S25	27	S26	33
S27	60	S28	24
S29	60	S30	48
S31	60	S32	60
S33	60	S34	60
S35	60	S36	36
S37	60	S38	36
S39	24	S40	24
Sum	1065		849
N	20		20
Mean	53.25		42.45

(13) In this table all the 'raw data' are given. This is not necessary, although the full data should be available in the appendix. Usually, some descriptive statistics and measures of central tendency and dispersion should be given. Graphical summaries like charts and graphs can usefully be included.

The data are scores, ordinal, nonparametric and of matched pairs design, and therefore a Wilcoxon test was applied. (See appendix 3 for calculations.)

$N = 15$

$T = 23.5$

Probability level – significant at 0.025

There seems to be no significant difference in the sentences given by males or females.

The mean sentences for each were as follows:

	Male	Female
Black	54.6	51.9
White	42.9	42
	48.75	46.95

(14) This table is interesting but addresses itself to an issue beyond that indicated by the hypothesis. The relevance of this will have to be established in the discussion.

Although the male's mean sentence is slightly higher.**(14)**

Discussion

As it can be seen from the results,**(15)** this experiment proved to be significant at a probability level of 0.025, as it was a one-tailed test. Therefore the null hypothesis should be rejected and the alternate one accepted, that the length of sentence given to black male attackers is significantly longer than that given to white male attackers. This seems to imply that the subjects were prejudiced when marking the length of sentence they believed necessary for the black attacker. The real question is why was this so? The subjects seemed to be prejudiced, but for what reason?

(15) A discussion should generally start with a clear reference to, and reflection on, the results of the study.

There has been a number of theories put forward to try and explain prejudice and perhaps one that may help to explain it in this context, is the 'conformity to group view' theory.**(16)** This suggests that if people live in a prejudiced society they too will become prejudiced because everyone else is. Our society is a prejudiced one, with blacks being treated as unequal and subjects in this experiment could have adopted this prejudice. If they have learnt to look down on blacks, they will think them more capable of committing a crime and perhaps more likely to commit a crime again and therefore that they deserve a longer sentence. Perhaps they believe that an attack by a black male would be even more frightening and unpleasant than an attack by a white male and so more punishment should be given.

(16) A reference to a specific theory writer would help here.

The 'scapegoat theory' could also help to explain why people may be prejudiced in this context. It suggests, that prejudice is the result of a certain situation and a minority is blamed for something that is not their fault. An example of this is blacks being blamed for taking jobs and causing the high unemployment level, by unemployed people. This blaming of a minority occurs in frustrated situations, such as being unemployed and can increase with frustration. This was shown in an experiment carried out by Miller and Bugelski (1948) in which they asked a group of subjects their feelings towards a minority group. Half were then shown a film and the other half given difficult, frustrating tests. When asked to state their feelings towards the group again, it was found that those subjects who had been given hard tests proved to be more prejudiced than before. It could be in this experiment that subjects, especially female ones, find the thought of being attacked frustrating and that their prejudice therefore grows.**(17)**

(17) This effectively links general theory to this particular study.

Obviously, the subjects used were not professional judges and it was therefore difficult for them to know how long a sentence to give. Twenty-one out of forty subjects sentenced the attacker to five years in prison, the longest sentence that could be given and perhaps the scale should have been longer to give them more choice. It could be that professional judges would not be prejudiced or biased in any way and with a jury it could be that the level of prejudice amongst the members of the jury is equalled out. But, a significant amount of prejudice was shown in this fairly simple experiment and it therefore seems quite likely that the same thing would take place in actual court cases, and this is not fair. Perhaps in cases where a black person is on trial a mixture of black and white people should be members of the jury, to balance out any prejudice among its members.

The experiment could have been inaccurate, due to the use of a matched pairs experimental design.**(18)** It could have been that those subjects given the description of the attack by the black male believed in harsher punishment than those given the description of the white attacker. This could not be helped, as it was impossible to use a related samples design, as if subjects had been given both of the descriptions they could have seen the difference of the black or white attacker.

(18) It is important to recognise that even a carefully constructed matched pairs design may contain unintentional errors in sampling.

In this experiment, the idea of the attacker being either black or white was given subtly, to try to stop subjects from being conscious that it was prejudice being tested. In the accounts, all other variables, such as the time or place of the attack, were kept constant, to make sure that just prejudice would be the cause of any difference in the length of sentences. Other studies could be carried out using the time of day as the variable to see if the attacker is given a shorter or longer sentence whether the attack is carried out at day or night.**(19)** The same experiment could be carried out with a different crime, such as stealing, used to see if there is any difference in the results. The idea of experimenting on prejudice could be taken further to see if there is a difference between what people say about being prejudiced and how they actually act, to see if the two correspond. Further experiments could also be carried out on prejudice reduction, as it is obvious that it exists.

(19) Extensions and developments of experiments should be envisaged, but need to be kept in the realm of the possible.

Conclusion This experiment has shown bias in prison sentencing due to racial prejudice.

References

Aronson E (1980) *The Social Animal* Freeman (Chapter 6)
Dobson C B *Understanding Psychology* Weidenfeld and Nicolson (p. 359–61)**(20)**

(20) More detail is needed in the references to allow location of the specific points mentioned in the introduction and discussion.

Appendix

1 The two cases of the attack.
2 The answer sheet.
3 A Wilcoxon test for Matched Pairs Design.
The two different cases of the attack one of which each subject would be shown.

A extract from a court report, taken from a September edition of the *Daily Mirror*:

"On Monday, July 6th, Mrs J Rawlings, aged 26 and a mother of two, was walking along Waterfall Road, Basildon at 10.00pm, when she was attacked and stabbed several times. She spent three days in the intensive care unit of Basildon Hospital. Several days later, the attacker, who she described a young, white male, was caught after an extensive police search of the area. The 20 year old attacker was later sentenced in the High Courts, Chelmsford."

How long do you think he should have been sentenced for?
Please mark on the scale below (with a cross)

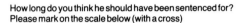

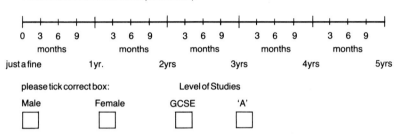

A Wilcoxon test for Matched Pairs Design

	Black	White	Difference	Rank	Signed Rank
1	36	60	−24	9 (−)	−9
2	42	60	−18	7 (−)	−7
3	60	60	0	−	
4	60	24	+36	12.5 (+)	
5	60	24	+36	12.5 (+)	
6	60	60	0	−	
7	60	9	+51	15 (+)	
8	60	24	+36	12.5 (+)	
9	48	60	−12	4.5 (−)	−4.5
10	60	48	+12	4.5 (+)	
11	60	48	+12	4.5 (+)	
12	48	51	− 3	1 (−)	−1
13	27	33	− 6	2 (−)	−2
14	60	24	+36	12.5 (+)	
15	60	48	+12	4.5 (+)	
16	60	60	0	−	
17	60	60	0	−	
18	60	36	+24	9 (+)	
19	60	36	+24	9 (+)	
20	24	24	0	−	

$N = 15$
$T = 23.5$
Probability level = significant at 0.025 for a one-tailed test

Revision and the examination

At various points during your course you will be revising for test essays. In preparation for the examination this process will begin in earnest. There are various techniques which you can use which will increase your effectiveness. Perhaps the main point to make is that *learning* your psychology notes and studies should not be left until a few weeks before the examination. As psychologists you will appreciate that we remember best what we really understand. Rote learning is much less efficient. Consequently, you should see the revision process as being part of your course from the beginning. We will look at revision, surviving 'exam nerves' and making the best use of your time in the examination room.

Revision

Good notes

Your revision will be aided by having made good notes throughout your course. These should not be too detailed, but must be accurate. If set out neatly, with the intelligent use of colour for underlining and 'highlight' pens for the important parts, then they will be easier to learn from and recall. It is never too early to start making extra notes around a topic, to back up class work. The more familiar you are with material the easier it is to learn.

Regular review

You will find it very helpful, if throughout your course you devote a small amount of time, regularly, to reviewing your recent notes. We remember relatively little of any lecture we may have attended. However, if we read over the notes we have taken, then they become more firmly lodged in the memory. This review should be conducted ideally, each day and each week. It need only last a minute or two, because all you have to do is to bring the points back to your attention. It counteracts the process of 'decay' in the memory.

Card system

Many students find keeping a card system is very helpful. On each card a brief summary of the main points of specific studies or experiments, is recorded. Small file cards are ideal. They may be used to revise from, and can ensure that you actually remember the key studies in the examination room, rather than having them on the 'tip of your tongue'.

Mnemonics

For many of the parts of the psychology syllabus, you will have to remember a series of studies or experiments. Often if you can recall the name of the experimenter, then the details will also come to mind. One simple technique is to come up with a mnemonic using the first letters of the names of psychologists. It is easier to recall one 'silly' word than eight or nine separate names. The process of working out a mnemonic also helps engrave the names on your memory. The figure overleaf shows how one enterprising student used the word perception itself, to act as a memory jog. Using a summary sheet like this, with little pictures, can also be an effective way of revising. Pictures involve the imaging, or right side of the brain. Putting pictures and ideas in a sequence means that we can move from one to the next by association. If you try out this technique (which rests on the same principle as the mind-maps used earlier in the book) you will discover that you can remember a sequence of material surprisingly effectively.

Plan for revision

The revision period should start several months prior to the examination. You should plan what you are going to revise and when, and draw up a schedule. Try to go over everything at least three times. The first time is to ensure that your notes are complete, and that you understand the ideas and the arguments. This phase is most important because you will not be able to effectively learn material that you do not understand. The second time you should put maximum effort into learning the material. Be ruthless with yourself, in checking that you really do recall the details of the studies and arguments that you have been learning. The third time is to check what you know, and to relearn what has not been memorised.

Be active

You will remember best what has gone actively through your mind. Don't just read through your notes. Close your file and verbally summarise (ie say out loud) the key ideas, or write them out. Make summaries of all the key points on a particular area, using boxes, colour, underlining, pictures, and any other techniques that will make them visually distinctive and memorable. Mind-maps would be particularly useful here as a way of drawing whole areas together in a structured way. Look at past questions, and either make detailed plans, or write out an answer in 43 to 45 minutes (the time available in the examination).

Work intensively for short periods separated by brief breaks. This maximises the primacy and recency effects, where we tend to remember best the beginnings and endings of activities.

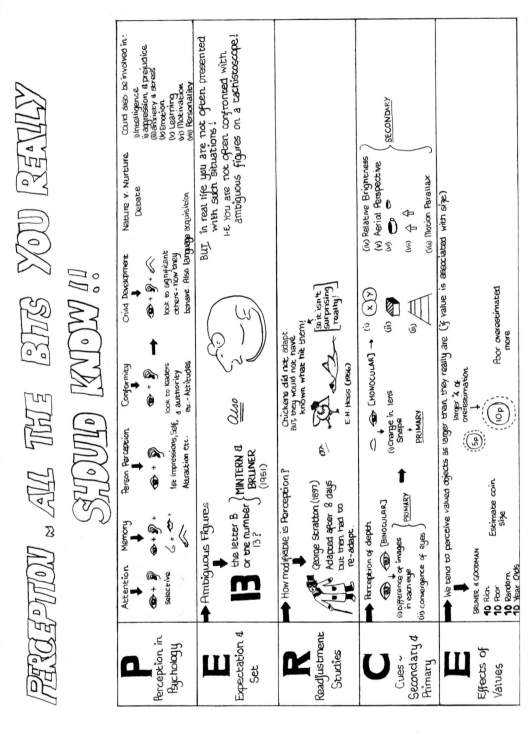

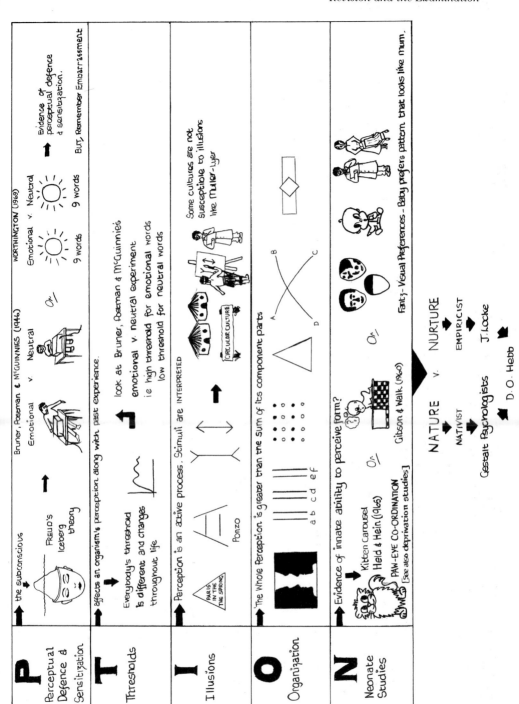

P — Perceptual Defence & Sensitization

↑ the subconscious

FREUD'S Iceberg theory

Bruner, Postman & McGuinnies (1946)

Emotional v. Neutral

Or

WORTHINGTON (1969)

Emotional v. Neutral

9 words — 9 words

↑ Evidence of perceptual defence & sensitization.

BUT, Remember Embarrassment

T — Thresholds

↑ Affects an organism's perception along with past experience.

Everybody's threshold is different and changes throughout life

Look at Bruner, Postman & McGuinnies' emotional v. neutral experiment ie high threshold for emotional words low threshold for neutral words

I — Illusions

↑ Perception is an active process. Stimuli are INTERPRETED

PARIS IN THE SPRING

Ponzo

ab cd ef

CIRCULAR CULTURE

Some cultures are not susceptible to illusions like Muller-Lyer

O — Organization

↑ "The Whole Perception is greater than the sum of its component parts"

Or

A B C D

Gestalt Psychologists

N — Neonate Studies

↑ Evidence of innate ability to perceive form?

Kitten Carousel Held & Hein (1965)

PAW-EYE CO-ORDINATION [See also deprivation studies]

Or

Gibson & Walk (1960)

Fantz — Visual Preferences — Baby prefers pattern that looks like mum.

NATURE v. NURTURE

NATIVIST — EMPIRICIST

Gestalt Psychologists → J. Locke

D.O. Hebb

Preparing for the methodology question

By running through the questions given in this book (pages 9–42) you will cover most of the main concepts that are likely to occur in the examination. So be sure that you *understand* the answers to each of these questions. Similarly, work through all the past questions of this type and make sure you can answer each part. The statistical part of the syllabus is not that difficult to grasp, *if* you are prepared to give it enough time, and to think about the concepts. This book gives a summary of the main ideas but you will need also to go to one of the introductory specialist books on statistics.

Surviving 'exam nerves'

A bit of adrenaline is no bad thing in the examination, as it can sharpen concentration. Being so nervous that you cannot think straight is of no value at all. There are ways that you can help yourself feel calm on the day.

Relaxation

It is worth practising simple relaxation techniques for some months prior to the examination, so that it becomes a habit. There are several books readily available to teach you how to relax (eg Jane Madders, *Stress and Relaxation*).

Breathing

Slow deep breaths affect the body, and can help it to calm down when it is distressed. Take a few deep breaths before going into the exam. Do so again once you are in your place. The very act of stopping, thinking about your breathing, and allowing your body to relax, can help you to avoid making silly mistakes through panicking.

Affirmations

A simple psychological technique can assist in this area. If you find a little voice in your head informing you that you are likely to fail/forget/go blank and so on, just say 'STOP'. Then replace that voice with one you consciously choose, saying a phrase like 'I will remember everything I need to' or 'I will be clear-headed and calm in the exam'.

Sleep and exercise

The exam season is a stressful time. Regular exercise will help you survive it, and also help you sleep. An evening walk can be very beneficial – especially if you use it as a time for *not* thinking about work. Don't burn the 'midnight candle' too much; it is counterproductive.

Psychology examination check list

Keep the following points in mind during the examination:
1. Read through the whole paper carefully.
2. Select your questions making sure that you follow the rubric on the paper.
3. Spend *equal* time on each question, this usually means about 43 to 44 minutes each, after reading the questions through.
4. Underline the key words on the question. Do *not* copy the question out onto the answer sheet.
5. Make a brief plan.
6. Check that the plan answers the question.
7. Start your essay from a point relating to a key issue in the question.
8. Link your essay paragraph by paragraph. Also link the main points regularly back to the question. Keep the paragraphs fairly short.
9. Back up any arguments with relevant examples or experiments.
10. Put dates where appropriate.
11. Put studies in historical sequence unless you have good reason to do otherwise. In other words your answer should show the development of ideas and arguments.
12. If you find yourself running out of time – or of ideas – check if there is another 'angle' to follow:
    theory/method

    another 'model' (eg behaviourism, humanistic psychology, social learning theory etc)

    an issue (eg reductionism; free will vs determinism; idiographic or nomothetic; ethical consideration etc)

    animal studies, if relevant
13. If you run out of time then complete the last question giving points you would have covered in telegraphic form.

Statistics Questions – Guidance on answers

The answers given here are not *model examination answers. Rather they are to help the student understand the content that must be covered in an examination answer. Generally what is required is a clear explanation, and an illustration – either from the stimulus material provided or an example from a relevant situation.*

Question 1

a) As they are frequency data, they can only be nominal.
b) The expected frequency is the score we would expect to obtain under the null hypothesis condition. In order to be valid it must equal or exceed five.
c) Degrees of freedom refers mathematically, to the number of scores in a result that can be varied, whilst the *parameters* – in effect, the totals – remain the same. In this case, the *df* is 1. Do you know the formulae for computing the *df* for both a Chi-square and a t-test?
d) It corrects for the error that can arise from using small samples, and *must* be used when the sample is under 25.
e) Here, 'p' refers to the probability and '$\leq$' can be expressed as 'equal to or less than'. A two-tailed test indicates that the experimenter does not predict the *direction* of the effect of the independent variable. Try putting both those ideas into a clear statement.
f) Descriptive statistics *describe* the data, whereas inferential statistics make *inferences* about the population that the sample (of people or scores) represents. It will be helpful to consider examples of both. One is looking back at the data already collected. The other, in effect, makes predictions. What is it making predictions about?

Question 2

a) Order effect, as the name suggests, is any extraneous influence produced by the order in which tests or activities are undertaken. Any possible effects need to be balanced out, or *counterbalanced*. You should be aware of how to do this when a group is undertaking more than two tests. Also, how should the group be allocated into sub-groups?
b) A Pearson's Product Moment test can only be applied when a scattergram indicates a straight line – not one that is curvilinear, or U-shaped.
c) A parametric test requires data that are of at least interval status, normally distributed, and where both samples have a similar variance.
d) The significance level *is* the chance of making a Type I error, so, the chance is 5 in 10,000.

104

e) A Type II error, is when a null hypothesis is accepted when it is false.
f) It is significant at the 0.025 level for a one-tailed test.

Question 3

a) The IV is whether the words are presented in categories or in random order. The DV is the number of words that are remembered under each condition.
b) The null hypothesis needs to reflect both the IV and the DV and to state that the group under the experimental condition (categories) will not have significantly different scores to the other group.
c) This refers to Popper's idea that in effect a scientist must test a conjecture (hypothesis) that is actually falsifiable. What is the implication if the hypothesis was *not* falsifiable?
d) There are two groups, randomly assigned rather than matched. So the design is *independent measures* or *between groups*.
e) Interval data, as the name suggests, are data that can be arranged on a scale of equal intervals. Test scores would usually be considered as interval. Ordinal data can, again as the name suggests, be put into rank order. Are interval data always ordinal?
f) Independent measures, testing for difference and with non-parametric data, hence Mann-Whitney.

Question 4

a) 34% or more accurately 34.15%
b) The middle line, bisecting the highest point on the distribution is the mean, median and mode. What are the other characteristics of the normal curve of distribution?
c) Standard deviation is one measure of *dispersion*. In other words it is a measure of the average 'spread' of scores around the mean. It summarises the average score of all the scores around the mean of those scores. What is its relationship to the variance? And in this example, what is the variance?
d) This score will be 100. It is the mean plus two standard deviations.
e) The probability is 2.3 times in 100 or $p = .023$.

Question 5

a) The sampling frame is the school roll.
b) The overall population is most accurately the pupils at this school – ie the same as the sampling frame. However, the population could be all 11 – 16 year old school children in this country. It would depend how *representative* the school itself was of other schools.
c) A random sample means that extraneous variables will tend to cancel each other out. The random sample could be selected by taking

every n^{th} name, by using random number tables or picking numbers that refer to the names, out of a hat.

Can you explain the difference between extraneous variables and confounding variables?

d) Demand characteristics are the inferences which the subject picks up about the purpose of the experiment and what is expected of him or her. In this case what might the pupils infer about the purpose of the experiment? How might this influence their response?

e) Two tests of reliability are the *test – retest* method and the *split – half* test. These would need to be explained.

f) Validity is when a test measures *truthfully*. In other words it measures what it is supposed to measure. It is the adequacy of a test to address the issue it is meant to address. This can be assessed in terms of its content, its results with known groups and its predictive ability. Consistency is not, in itself, a measure of validity, but of reliability. So a reliable test *may* be consistently invalid!

Question 6

a) In this experiment your subjects perform under two conditions. This is therefore a *repeated measures* design.

b) You cannot assume that the attitude scale is treated by the subjects in the same way, nor that the steps between scores are of equal value. Hence, the data are only of *ordinal* status, because you can put them in rank order.

c) The experimental hypothesis must include the IV and the DV and specify the relationship between them. In this case the IV is the soap operas, and the DV is the rating given to them. As you are unsure which will prove more popular you just need to specify that there will be a significant difference in the scores on the attitude scale. The hypothesis therefore has to be two-tailed.

d) The level of significance achieved for a two-tailed test is always half that for a one-tailed test. In other words if it is of borderline significance for a two-tailed test, it will be significant for a one-tailed test.